ADMINSTRATIVE REMEDIES IN PRISONS

BY

JUSTIN THRASHER[1]
ANANT KUMAR TRIPATI[2]

Adminstrative Remedies In Prisons

Copyright © 2017 By Justin Thrasher and Anant Kumar Tripati

All rights Reserved. No part of this book may be reproduced or transmitted in any form by any means, graphic, electronic or mechanical including photocopying, recording, taping or by any information storage or retrieval system without written permission from publisher. The purpose of this book is to inform, educate and entertain. Although every precaution has been taken in preparation of this book, there may be errors or omissions. Neither is any liability assumed for damages resulting, directly or indirectly, from the use of this information contained within this book.

Libarary of Congress Cataloging-in-Publication Data
Adminstrative Remedies in Prisons
This book has been published and made available as an e-book.

Published by:
SureShot Books Publishing LLC
P.O. Box 924
Nyack, New York 10960
www.sureshotbooks.com
ISBN : 978-1-947170-21-6

TABLE OF CONTENTS

Overview of the Research 1

Introduction 2

A Judge's View of Pro Se Litigation... 3

The Dilemma 5

Pleading Requirements for Pro Se Litigants
Violate Federal Rules 6

Reaction to the Schisms and Interpretative Conflicts:
Emergence of Multiple Approaches to Pro Se Litigation 10

Enhanced Liberal Construction for Pro Se Litigants..................... 12

The Rise in Subjectivity 14

The Lessons Learned from the Plra and Aedpa............................ 18

Proper Interpretation and the Diminished Importance of
HAINES V. KERNER 20

The Law on Prisoner Complaints Under 1983 21

Law on Exhaustion 31

Lawsuits on Healthcare 56

Victims Targeted by Healthcare Providers.................................... 61

Arizona Class Action Law Suit Settlement 64

Procedural History 97

Statement of Facts 98

Defendants' Audits Document A Broken System 99

Experts Find System Flawed 109

Judicial Decisions On Exhaustion 140

Judicial Decisions on Prson Healthcare 167

Conclusion 192

References 193

The question we present is why is there an increase in prisoner litigation and how may it be reduced. Utilizing conceptual, theoretical and normative approaches we believe evidence shows that Congress as well as state legislators must change the law to require that administrative remedy procedures be both effective and adequate. Examination of the litigation against prison authorities, healthcare providers Corizon Inc and Wexford Health Sources show that had administrative remedies been effective and adequate, litigation would have been avoided. It is clear from examining these litigation that prison authorities refuse to administratively resolve issues, but instead force litigation by inmates, thereby tying up substantial agency, judicial and individual resources. Their lawyers, as their insurance companies pay claims, force litigation.

OVERVIEW OF THE RESEARCH

ADMINISTRATIVE REMEDIES ARE UNAVAILABLE WHEN STATE AUTHORITIES HAVE REFUSED TO EXERCISE THEIR AUTHORITY TO CORRECT CONTINUING VIOLATIONS—CASE STUDTY OF U.S. PRISONS, CORIZON LLC AND WEXFORD HEALTH SOURCES INC.

INTRODUCTION

Prison authorities in the United States[3] use the administrative remedy process as a vehicle to delay/deny treatment to inmates for their serious medical needs and other conditions. This paper shows why courts should not require prisoners to utilize the administrative remedy process when prison authorities have a systemic practice of not taking corrective actions.[4]

A JUDGE'S VIEW OF PRO SE LITIGATION

HON. ROBERT BACHARACH[*] LYN ENTZEROTH writes in theory the law creates impersonal rules of behavior that courts apply in an identical fashion regardless of the litigant.[5] Ideally, the powerful and powerless can expect to follow the same rules of law and procedure in any courtroom. Through neutral rules of practice and procedure, the courts seek to assure an equal opportunity for a full and fair hearing to all parties. Of course, the world is not perfect and there are obvious variables ranging from the lawyers' abilities, to the financial wherewithal of the parties that might affect the process of litigation. Yet, courts could apply their rules in a similar fashion to all with the hope that such a system will produce a just result.

The morass of approaches to pro se litigation reflects a long-standing ambivalence over pleading standards and the judge's role in the adversarial process. As pleading standards softened, courts struggled with how to address fanciful suits brought by unrepresented parties. With this internal struggle, judges understandably hoped to relieve pro se litigants of endless procedural traps when the underlying claims appeared meritorious. In this setting, the Supreme Court innocuously noted the claimant's pro se status in *Haines v. Kerner*, and lower courts set out to use this phrase to vindicate an infinite set of views about how to assess pleading standards and how to help unrepresented parties navigate various procedural traps. These efforts proved not only futile, but also counter-productive. In the process, the courts compromised their own neutrality and limited role.

The recent sharpening of pleading standards should relieve judges of these conflicts. Judges no longer enjoy open license to devise their own ways of dealing with implausible suits by pro se litigants. The inevitable and long overdue result is the judiciary's return to its traditional function as the neutral arbiter of fairness in the litigation process. Like everyone else, some pro se litigants will achieve fair results and others will not, but equality in treatment will at least ensure fairness in the process for everyone.

Somewhere this ideal of neutrality has derailed in favor of an incongruous, ad hoc set of rules applicable only to pro se litigants.[2] While courts arguably intended some of these rules to benefit the pro se litigant and to ease the disadvantage of proceeding without counsel, in practice, even benign rules have worked to disfavor or even punish the pro se litigant. The result is that ad hoc rules designed to protect pro se litigants are often doing just the opposite. This Article endeavors to (1) trace the set of rules that apply uniquely to pro se litigants, (2) explore how those rules derailed, and (3) suggest a path for restoration of the impersonal ideal that once underlay the legal fabric of American law.

THE DILEMMA

The schism that has developed in the treatment of pro se litigation is the byproduct of two conflicting goals used in the evaluation of pro se pleadings. The first objective involves the measures used to assess whether the pleading sufficiently states a claim for relief.[3] Part of this objective seeks to assure that mere procedural technicalities do not trip up the unwary litigant.[6] The second, somewhat incongruous goal, deals with the basic notion that both the represented and unrepresented must follow the same procedural rules.[7]

PLEADING REQUIREMENTS FOR PRO SE LITIGANTS VIOLATE FEDERAL RULES

The first objective in the evaluation of pleadings is captured in the well-known terms of Federal Rule of Civil Procedure (Rule) 8(a)(2), which provides that a pleading setting out a claim for relief need only contain "a short and plain statement of the claim showing that the pleader is entitled to relief."[8] This liberal pleading requirement reflects a long-established policy move away from the technical or stylized pleading forms of earlier common law practice.[9] Under the Rules, the function of pleading a claim for relief[10] is to give sufficient notice to the adverse party[11] even if the plaintiff fails to adequately identify the legal theory for relief or detail relevant facts.[12]

Over fifty years ago the Supreme Court in *Conley v. Gibson*[13] set out to create a broad, principled method for judges to use in assessing the facial validity of a complaint based on the language and purpose of the liberalized system of notice pleading.[14] The oft-quoted language of *Conley* provides: "[W]e follow, of course, the accepted rule that a complaint should not be dismissed for failure to state a claim unless it appears beyond doubt that the plaintiff can prove no set of facts in support of his claim which would entitle him to relief."[15]

Following *Conley*, the conventional wisdom was that a pleading could pass muster as long as the claimant could prove any set of facts, consistent with the complaint, which might justify relief. While this liberal standard of pleading interpretation theoretically prevented dismissal of a complaint due simply to defects in form or in artful pleading style, critics asserted that under this broad standard virtually any complaint or claim could survive a motion to dismiss.Indeed, this liberal standard of pleading review would permit many implausible claims to survive a motion to dismiss. Moreover, since the system allowed implausible claims to survive the pleading stage of litigation, the stated test rarely commanded the degree of obedience from the courts that one would have expected.

Virtually from the start, courts devised inroads which would permit more careful scrutiny of claims regarded as implausible.[16] For example while federal courts acknowledged the extraordinarily liberal pleading standard articulated in *Conley*, federal courts also: (1) interjected a requirement that the claimant have a "'reasonably founded hope that the [discovery] process [would] reveal relevant evidence' to support [the] claim";[17] (2) declined to assume facts not alleged;[18] (3) rejected allegations in a complaint that were regarded as "conclusory" or "conjectural";[19] and (4) emphasized that Rule 8 requires "that the 'plain statement' possess enough heft to 'sho[w]' that the pleader is entitled to relief.'"[20] The inconsistency between the language of *Conley* and the reality of practice proved transparent, as courts frequently gave lip-service to *Conley*'s sweeping language while creating more and more ways to restrict litigation regarded as implausible or frivolous.[21] This phenomenon proved to be particularly pronounced in prisoner litigation, where many ad hoc, unskilled claimants proceeded pro se and "unfortunately provided conflicting guideposts" and stating that the Supreme Court had "elsewhere hinted that sometimes more particularity in pleading [could] be required");[22]

The rise of modern prisoner litigation can be traced to the general expansion of civil rights litigation that occurred during the 1960s and 1970s[23] By the mid-1960s, federal courts provided remedies to prisoners seeking relief from unconstitutional prison conditions under 42 U.S.C. § 1983.[24] By 1973, the Court acknowledged "recent decisions upholding the right of state prisoners to bring federal civil rights actions to challenge the conditions of their confinement."[25]

Some prisoner litigation involves class action suits brought against prison officials or other appropriate authorities for large-scale, systemic, and supervised injunctions against unconstitutional conditions of confinement[26]

Other prison litigation involves a single prisoner, often proceeding pro se, seeking injunctive or monetary redress for individual grievances such as use of excessive force by prison officials, unconstitutional living conditions, risk of harm from other prisoners, and deliberate indifference to medical needs.[27]

With continued attention to implausible claims, the Supreme Court recently elevated the legal consequences of skepticism.[28] In doing so, the Supreme Court treated the fifty-year-old *Conley* standard as if it were but a relic[29] and held that frequently raised claims that courts deemed implausible or frivolous.[30] Rather than confront this disconnect between reality and the pleading ideal, avoidance became a particularly powerful incentive as courts struggled to confront a rapid rise in prisoner litigation. The result was that many claims regarded as implausible, nonetheless, easily survived the conventional test for dismissal.[31]

The schism in American law also found expression in conflicting modes of enforcement for procedural rules that were seemingly mandatory for all litigants. Virtually all judges paid lip-service to the notion that pro se litigants had to follow generally applicable procedural rules notwithstanding the litigant's frequent lack of legal training, education, and/or resources.[32] However, the inflexibility of this view implicates identical treatment for both plausible and implausible claims. The problem is that pro se litigants often lack the knowledge or experience to discern differences in the requirements of various procedural rules,[33] such as the variety of responses required for an answer to a motion to dismiss or a motion for summary judgment.[34] This lack of knowledge could result in dismissal of an otherwise meritorious claim. Skeptical of the rigidity in this approach, with identical treatment of counseled and uncounseled litigants, courts struggled to create ways for plausible inmate suits to survive despite procedural irregularities.

One such method involved the creation of ad hoc requirements for judges to advise litigants about the rules before enforcing them.[35] While some courts have declined to require such advice,[36] even those courts have devised ways of protecting pro se litigants from procedural mishaps.[37] For example, one court recognized the power to dismiss claims that violate Rule 8, but suggested that judges should not order dismissal of pro se complaints unless they have explained for a "lay person . . . what judges and lawyers mean when speaking of a short and plain statement consistent with Rule 8."[38] In contrast, attorneys violating the rule do not receive the same judicial advice before their suits are dismissed.[39]

REACTION TO THE SCHISMS AND INTERPRETATIVE CONFLICTS: EMERGENCE OF MULTIPLE APPROACHES TO PRO SE LITIGATION

The schisms in the approaches to dismissal and procedural compliance have coalesced in a multi-faceted blend in how judges approach pro se litigation. The liberality of the standard for dismissal would permit innumerable suits to proceed despite deep skepticism of their underlying merit. The recently-imposed test of plausibility[40] creates an opportunity for courts to impose their own beliefs about the merit of the underlying suit despite the superficial liberality of the standard for dismissal. The continuum between the flexibility of Rule 8 and the subjective ingredient of plausibility allows the courts to form ad hoc devices to impose their own beliefs in a system supposedly based on objectivity and uniformity.

Even worse, a forum predicated on blind justice has evolved into a system that reflects a keen eye for the persona of the litigant.[41] Certain rules govern pro se litigants, while other rules govern parties represented by lawyers. Sometimes the pro se litigants are favored;[42] sometimes they are disfavored.[43] Moreover, sometimes the pro se litigants are lawyers,[44] resulting in either foolish paternalism or unprincipled assessments of their legal ability[45]. The multiplicity of interpretative approaches and degrees of judicial intervention derive from the array of subjective [46] standards applied to review of pleadings, which, in turn, evolve from judicial efforts[47] to blend disparate tests, inconsistent approaches to procedural requirements, and varying attitudes towards pro se litigation.

With increasing subjectivity, courts have placed their gloss on various procedural rules. The opportunity to do so has resulted from the loosening of principle and elevation of the judge's dual role as the guardian and gatekeeper of pro se litigation.[48]

ENHANCED LIBERAL CONSTRUCTION FOR PRO SE LITIGANTS

The dual rule of the judge is manifest in how courts have treated an otherwise innocuous passage in the *Haines v. Kerner*[49] per curiam opinion issued thirty-six years ago. In *Haines*, the Supreme Court applied the *Conley* pleading standard[51] for review of the viability of complaints in light of the litigant's pro se status.[50] In that context, the *Haines* Court stated:

Whatever may be the limits on the scope of inquiry of courts into the internal administration of prisons, allegations such as those asserted by petitioner, however in artfully pleaded, are sufficient to call for the opportunity to offer supporting evidence. We cannot say with assurance that under the allegations of the pro se complaint, which we hold to less stringent standards than formal pleadings drafted by lawyers, it appears "beyond doubt that the plaintiff can prove no set of facts in support of his claim which would entitle him to relief."[51]

Although the *Haines* Court relaxed the pleading standard for the pro se plaintiff, the Court did not define the degree of relaxation in comparison to the pro se liberal notice pleading rules applicable to all litigants in Rule 8.

With the deterioration in objective standards and the intensification of judges' reliance on their own beliefs, the innocuous passage in *Haines* has become a mirror for courts to act on their own perceptions of the plausibility of the underlying litigation.[52] Ideally, under *Haines*, plausible claims proceed while implausible ones do not. The trouble is that plausibility is inherently subjective and judges' likely gauge "plausibility" differently based on their ideologies, attitudes, and experiences.

Perhaps echoing the policy of protection of prisoners and liberal construction of such pro se pleadings, the District Court for Massachusetts stated:

As a marginalized group, prisoners are especially apt to require judicial protection. The United States has both a strong commitment to human rights and a clear history of human rights violations against prisoners, making such protection particularly appropriate and necessary. In light of these legal and empirical factors, courts should read prisoner petitions generously, give them careful consideration, and resolve statutory ambiguities in prisoners' favor.[53]

Some commentators have expressed concern that pro se pleadings actually are treated more harshly than other pleadings, apparently in an effort to clear court dockets of unwanted litigation involving pro se inmates. Professor Howard Eisenberg observes:

Although courts routinely pay lip service to the liberal construction of pro se pleadings, as required by the Supreme Court in *Kerner*, there is a nagging concern among those few independent persons who have reviewed prisoner cases that the district courts are actually applying very different criteria when trying to rid their docket of pesky prisoner litigation. One commentator, who reviewed only reported district and courts of appeal decisions, found that a significant number of courts have applied stringent pleading standards to pro se plaintiffs, ignoring the explicit directions of *Haines v. Kerner* or "giving its language only superficial acknowledgment."[54]

THE RISE IN SUBJECTIVITY

Without objective standards to provide guidance, courts have chosen to decide for themselves which pro se cases are plausible and which are not.[57] Not surprisingly, judges have erected their own artifices to allow pro se cases to survive an infinite variety of procedural traps[55].

Seeking to relieve pro se litigants of various procedural traps, courts have created new, unanticipated dangers. Tangibly, such relief has resulted in unintended consequences for the litigants chosen for favorable treatment. Intangibly, judicial benevolence has resulted in a softening of the distinction between advocacy and neutrality. For example, courts have utilized ad hoc rules to interpret or advance a pro se litigant's perceived grievance, such as recharacterizing suits under 42 U.S.C. § 1983 as habeas petitions, advising litigants how to comply with rules, and warning litigants of the need to comply with procedural requirements. With the emergence of these rules, courts frequently struggle to maintain their neutrality when called on to perform functions typically associated with advocacy. Judicial efforts to forecast the effects of various constructions on the pro se litigant illustrate this loss in objectivity. Without legislative power, the judiciary is at a loss to predict these effects. Two examples arose in 1995 and 1996 with Congress's enactment of the Prison Litigation Reform Act of 1995 (PLRA)[56] and the Antiterrorism and Effective Death Penalty Act of 1996 (AEDPA).[57] The two laws brought to the surface the futility and danger of compensating for a party's lack of legal representation.

With the PLRA, Congress hoped to curtail the flood of inmate litigation. In many ways, the PLRA reflected legislative frustration with the rise of prisoner litigation and the perceived intrusion of the federal judiciary in the operation of state prison systems. That frustration is evident in the statutory hurdles facing inmates who seek judicial review of prison conditions. Two important components of this effort were (1) the requirement of administrative exhaustion of claims[58] and (2) restrictions on inmates' eligibility for pauper status.[59]

The PLRA requires inmates to exhaust available administrative remedies before suing under federal law based on conditions within the prison.[60] The exhaustion provision creates tension with twenty-four years of precedent, originating in *Haines v. Kerner*,[61] in which federal courts had struggled to identify the causes of action encompassed in many prisoner complaints.[62]

Federal courts have long discarded the ancient requirement for a litigant to identify his legal theories in the complaint.[63] As a result, even for parties enjoying legal representation, the courts read into the complaint all causes of action fairly encompassed by the pleader's factual allegations.[64] This exercise often proves to be simple when the plaintiff enjoys legal representation,[65] but the process becomes far more problematic when the plaintiff lacks legal training or representation. In the absence of such training or representation, litigants often try to express their claims without the ability to pinpoint the misdeeds that are actionable. Deciphering these complaints frequently required courts to decide whether to err on the side of a narrow construction or a generous one. One option involved strict adherence to in artful and, perhaps, unintended language of the pro se complaint itself.[66] Another option was to construe the complaint to fairly encompass all claims fairly raised by the pro se litigant's pleading.[67] Prior to 1996, courts had little reason to read complaints narrowly. With generous construction, courts could ferret out the viable claims, and if the courts proved overly generous in their construction, pro se litigants could drop any claims that they had not intended to insert. As a result, judges often interpreted pro se complaints to include whatever legal theories could be encompassed by the plaintiff's factual allegations.[68]

This type of construction seemed reasonable prior to 1996 and consistent with the judiciary's commitment to fairness and the elevation of substance over form. However, this liberal construction practice ultimately collided with the PLRA exhaustion requirement[69] Indeed, with the passage of the PLRA, a court's commitment to generous construction often proved unfair to the very people it intended to help.

For example, until recently, some courts "generously" read legal claims into complaints only to dismiss the entire action if the plaintiff failed to exhaust even a single theory.[70] The anomaly was that the theory might have been unexhausted only because the pro se litigant had not intended to assert it in the litigation as a separate cause of action. Benign in purpose, proactive construction of pro se complaints has proved far from benign in result.

The same has often been true even in those courts that decline to dismiss the entire action when some of the claims were exhausted and some were not.[71] In addition to requiring administrative exhaustion, Congress intensified the requirements for pauper status for prisoners who had filed baseless lawsuits.[72] Congress did so by treating dismissals for "frivolousness" or "failure to state a valid claim" as "strikes."[73] A prisoner could accumulate three "strikes" without a penalty, but once the inmate obtained three "strikes," he could only gain pauper status upon a showing that he was in imminent risk of serious bodily harm.[74]

With the statutory change, courts have struggled to determine when a "strike" has taken place. Some courts conclude that a "strike" occurs when a trial court dismisses even a single cause of action for frivolousness or failure to state a valid claim. In these courts, deciphering a pro se party's complaint can often create hidden consequences extending far beyond the case itself. For example, a pro se party could, hypothetically, assert five claims, prevail on four, and suffer dismissal of one. The lone dismissal could forever jeopardize pauper status for the litigant even though he had prevailed in the suit. In these circumstances, the pro se litigant would suffer even without a hint of having abused his pauper status.

The danger is heightened by the treacherous task of deciding which claims were intended by the plaintiff and which were not. In the hypothetical situation, the pro se litigant might never have intended to assert the single cause of action that was dismissed. The courts, benign in purpose, might be forever penalizing the same litigants who were the intended beneficiaries of such judicial generosity.

THE LESSONS LEARNED FROM THE PLRA AND AEDPA

With this intangible loss of a judge's neutrality, the courts may be creating unintended penalties for the litigants who the courts are paradoxically trying to help. The 1996 changes in the PLRA and AEDPA illustrate these dangers. Remedies, and second and the 1996 amendments governing pauper status,[75] exhaustion of administrative successive habeas petitions and motions under 28 U.S.C. § 2255 created new consequences for prior recipients of judicial paternalism. In bestowing these acts of paternalism, the courts may not have foreseen the changes ultimately taking place in 1996. Moreover, the courts currently engaging in judicial paternalism may not foresee future changes.

There is no definitive solution to the minefield of potential problems wrought by benevolence for pro se litigants. The futility is seen in the courts' current efforts to alleviate these problems through the invention of a requirement for warnings or a unilateral determination about the fairness of treating a petition or motion as second or successive once another court has engaged in recharacterization.[76] The minefield of dilemmas results from the slippage in the courts' appreciation for the adversarial system. As the arbiters of the system, judges often view the ultimate objective as fairness.[77] The difficulty arises, however, from an occasional failure to distinguish between fairness of the process and fairness of individual results.[78] As judges frequently recognize, a pro se litigant ordinarily lacks the knowledge and ability of his opposing attorney. However, even when both sides are represented, the attorneys are often unequal in ability,[79] just as some witnesses, clients, and jurors are better than others.[80] As one federal appellate judge remarked:

Trials are not clinical investigations, performed under laboratory conditions. They are human confrontations, subject to all the normal risks of human error and with the risks compounded by the dramatic intensity of the event, the contentiousness of the adversary process, and the distortions that sometimes arise from disparity in talent and resources of the contending sides.[81]

The effort to equalize adversarial ability is a futile endeavor, but the hopelessness of the task is not the greatest danger. Instead, the greater danger is the loosening of the well-designed constraints on the role of the judiciary in the adversarial process. Judges are not advocates or advisors. When judges adopt these roles, they violate deeply embedded legal principles. For example, advocacy runs afoul of the judge's duty of impartiality.[82] Additionally, giving legal advice is prohibited by multiple canons of judicial conduct.[83] Finally, warnings to litigants closely resemble the sort of "advisory opinions" prohibited in Article III of the United States Constitution.[84] The courts' attempts to advocate, counsel, and warn stem from an admirable objective—fairness. But the judge's role in our system is to ensure fairness of the process rather than fairness to an individual case.[85] Otherwise, the judge's task is one of futility because endless inequities exist in any case.

PROPER INTERPRETATION AND THE DIMINISHED IMPORTANCE OF *HAINES V. KERNER*

To reverse the thirty-six year distortion of *Haines*, courts must understand the source. Many courts have afforded special treatment to equalize the legal resources available to litigants.[86] Equalization of resources would require participation of the judge as an advocate and advisor. With this loss in neutrality, courts risk unintended problems for pro se litigants and the assumption of legislative roles. The key to construction of pro se pleadings involves an understanding of what the litigant has said.[87] When a litigant is unrepresented, he may be unable to clearly express himself to a court. As a result, *Haines* required the courts to show some flexibility in their interpretation of a pro se litigant's pleadings.[88] Courts have ample resources available to determine the pro se party's intent. For example, in the Fifth Circuit, courts conduct *Spears* hearings[89] to assist in screening prisoner complaints for frivolousness or failure to state a valid claim.[90] These proceedings can easily be modified to permit the judge to inquire into the pleader's intent. Once the court learns the pleader's intent, the task of interpretation is complete. Further steps to help the pro se litigant involve advocacy and counsel rather than interpretation. Such steps are, therefore, inappropriate.

THE LAW ON PRISONER COMPLAINTS UNDER 1983

❡❡ [A] [§ 1983] suit against a state official in his or her official capacity is not a suit against the official but rather is a suit against the official's office," i.e., against the State.[91] The State is not a "person" amenable to suit under § 1983. Id. The state and its agencies are immune from suit pursuant to the Eleventh Amendment.[92] The only exceptions to a state's immunity are (1) if the state has consented to suit or (2) if Congress has properly abrogated a state's immunity.[93] The only other exception is when the Ex parte Young exception applies. See S&M Brands, 527 F.3d at 507. Under this exception, "a federal court can issue prospective injunctive and declaratory relief compelling a state official to comply with federal law." Id. (quoting Will, 491 U.S. at 71 & n.10).

A request for injunctive relief requires that a plaintiff make a showing of "real or immediate threat" of injury.[94] Plaintiff is entitled to preliminary injunctive relief only if he/she shows either: "(1) a likelihood of success on the merits and the possibility of irreparable injury; or (2) the existence of serious questions going to the merits and the balance of hardships tipping in [the movant's] favor."[95] Under either formulation of the test, the movant must demonstrate a significant threat of irreparable injury.[96]

Further, in unusual circumstances where the preliminary injunction relates to the inmate's access to the district court, the district court need not consider the merits of the underlying complaint in considering whether to grant a preliminary injunction.[97]

The purpose of preliminary injunctive relief is to preserve the status quo or to prevent irreparable injury pending the resolution of the underlying claim on the merits. Therefore, the party seeking preliminary injunctive relief "must necessarily establish a relationship between the injury claimed in the motion and the conduct asserted in the complaint."[98] Thus, Plaintiff must ordinarily seek injunctive relief related to the merits of his underlying claim. "A district court should not issue an injunction when the injunction in question is not of the same character, and deals with a matter lying wholly outside the issues in the suit."[99]

To state a claim under § 1983 against a private entity performing a traditional public function, such as providing medical care in a prison, a plaintiff must allege facts to support that his constitutional rights were violated as a result of a policy, decision, or custom promulgated or endorsed by the private entity.[100] Because there is no respondeat superior liability under § 1983, a defendant's position as the employer of someone who allegedly violated a plaintiff's constitutional rights. , "[A] plaintiff must allege facts, not simply conclusions, that show that an individual was personally involved in the deprivation of his civil rights."[101] For an individual to be liable in his official capacity, a plaintiff must allege that the official acted as a result of a policy, practice, or custom. [102] Further, there is no respondeat superior liability under § 1983, so a defendant's position as the supervisor of someone who allegedly violated a plaintiff's constitutional rights does not make him liable. [103] A supervisor in his individual capacity "is only liable for constitutional violations of his subordinates if the supervisor participated in or directed the violations, or knew of the violations and failed to act to prevent them." Taylor, 880 F.2d at 1045. To state a claim for failure to train, a plaintiff must allege facts to support that the alleged failure amounted to deliberate indifference.[104] A plaintiff must allege facts to support that not only was particular training inadequate, but also that such inadequacy was the result of "a 'deliberate' or 'conscious' choice" on the part of the defendant. Id. at 1213-14;[105]

As a general matter, government officials may not be held liable for the unconstitutional conduct of their subordinates under a theory of respondeat superior or vicarious liability.[106] A claimed constitutional violation must be based upon active unconstitutional behavior.[107] The acts of one's subordinates are not enough, nor can supervisory liability be based upon the mere failure to act.[108] "[A] plaintiff must plead that each Government-official defendant, through the official's own individual actions, has violated the Constitution." *Iqbal, 556 U.S. at 676*. Liability under ~ 1983 may not be imposed simply because a supervising official denied an administrative grievance or failed to act on information contained in a grievance.[109]

A private citizen "lacks a judicially cognizable interest in the prosecution or nonprosecution of another."[110] "The failure to conduct a full and fair investigation and prosecution of an alleged crime does not state a claim unless there is a violation of another recognized constitutional right."[111] Plaintiff does not have a constitutional right to have prison officials effectively investigate his grievances, as he does not have a right to an effective grievance procedure.[112] Moreover, a prison official's failure to conduct an investigation into a claim of misconduct does not rise to the level of involvement that would make the official liable for such misconduct.[113] *U.S. Const. amend. VIII*. The *Eighth Amendment* obligates prison authorities to provide medical care to incarcerated individuals, as a failure to provide such care would be inconsistent with contemporary standards of decency.[114] The *Eighth Amendment* is violated when a prison official is deliberately indifferent to the serious medical needs of a prisoner. *Id. at 104-05*;[115]

To support a *§ 1983* claim against a private entity[116] performing a traditional public function, such as providing medical care to prisoners, a plaintiff must allege facts to support that his constitutional rights were violated as a result of a policy, decision, or custom promulgated or endorsed by the private entity. A private entity is not liable simply because it employed individuals who allegedly violated a plaintiff's constitutional rights. *See Tsao, 698 F.3d at 1139.* Therefore, a private entity can only be held liable under *§ 1983* for its employees' civil rights deprivations if plaintiff can show that an official policy or custom caused the constitutional violation.[117]

The requisite elements of a *§ 1983* claim against a private entity performing a state function are: (1) the plaintiff was deprived of a constitutional right; (2) the entity had a policy or custom; (3) the policy or custom amounted to deliberate indifference to the plaintiff's constitutional right; and (4) the policy or custom was the moving force behind the constitutional violation.[118] The limitations to liability established in *Monell* apply even where the plaintiff seeks only prospective relief and not money damages.[119]

Under the *Eighth Amendment* standard, a prisoner must demonstrate "deliberate indifference to serious medical needs."[120] There are two prongs to the deliberate-indifference analysis: an objective standard and a subjective standard. First, a prisoner must show a "serious medical need." *Jett, 439 F.3d at 1096* (citations omitted). A "'serious' medical need exists if the failure to treat a prisoner's condition could result in[121] further significant injury or the 'unnecessary and wanton infliction of pain.'" Examples of indications that a prisoner has a serious medical need include "[t]he existence of an injury that a reasonable doctor or patient would find important and worthy of comment or treatment; the presence of a medical condition that significantly affects an individual's daily activities; or the existence of chronic and substantial pain." *McGuckin, 974 F.2d at 1059-60.*

Second, a prisoner must show that the defendant's response to that need was deliberately indifferent. *Jett, 439 F.3d at 1096.* An official acts with deliberate indifference if he "knows of and disregards an excessive risk to inmate health or safety; the official must both be aware of facts from which the inference could be drawn that a substantial risk of serious harm exists, and he must also draw the inference." *Farmer, 511 U.S. at 837.* "Prison officials are deliberately indifferent to a prisoner's serious medical needs when they deny, delay, or intentionally interfere with medical treatment,"[122] or when they fail to respond to a prisoner's pain or possible medical need. *Jett, 439 F.3d at 1096.* But the deliberate-indifference doctrine is limited; an inadvertent failure to provide adequate medical care or negligence in diagnosing or treating a medical condition does not support an *Eighth Amendment* claim.[123] Further, a mere difference in medical opinion does not establish deliberate indifference.[124]

Where the plaintiff seeks injunctive relief to prevent a substantial risk of serious injury from becoming actual harm, the deliberate indifference determination is based on the defendant's current conduct. *Farmer, 511 U.S. at 845.* Thus, to survive summary judgment, the plaintiff "must come forward with evidence from which it can be inferred that the defendant-officials were at the time suit was filed, and are at the time of summary judgment, knowingly and unreasonably disregarding an objectively intolerable risk of harm, and that they will continue to do so[.]" *Id. at 846.*

Even if deliberate indifference is shown, to support an *Eighth Amendment* claim, the prisoner must demonstrate harm caused by the indifference[125] And to support a preliminary injunction for specific medical treatment, the plaintiff must demonstrate ongoing harm or the present threat of irreparable injury.[126] Refusing to follow the advice of a treating specialist may evidence deliberate indifference.[127] In addition, a failure to competently treat a serious medical condition, even if some treatment is prescribed, may constitute deliberate indifference in a particular case.[128]

Not every claim by a prisoner relating to inadequate medical treatment states a violation of the *Eighth* or *Fourteenth Amendment*. To state a *§ 1983* medical claim, a plaintiff must show that the defendants acted with "deliberate indifference to serious medical needs."[129] A plaintiff must show (1) a "serious medical need" by demonstrating that failure to treat the condition could result in further significant injury or the unnecessary and wanton infliction of pain and (2) the defendant's response was deliberately indifferent. *Jett, 439 F.3d at 1096* (quotations omitted).

"Deliberate indifference is a high legal standard."[130] To act with deliberate indifference, a prison official must both know of and disregard an excessive risk to inmate health; "the official must both be aware of facts from which the inference could be drawn that a substantial risk of serious harm exists, and he must also draw the inference."[131] Deliberate indifference in the medical context may be shown by a purposeful act or failure to respond to a prisoner's pain or possible medical need and harm caused by the indifference. *Jett, 439 F.3d at 1096*. Deliberate indifference may also be shown when a prison official intentionally denies, delays, or interferes with medical treatment or by the way prison doctors respond to the prisoner's medical needs. *Estelle, 429 U.S. at 104-05; Jett, 439 F.3d at 1096*.

Criticisms of the PLRA

Kyle T. Sullivan,[132]The need for revision of the PLRA is clear from a review of its discrete provisions and their cumulative effect, but these criticisms alone are not enough.[133] Lasting reform demands a more exacting inquiry into the policy missteps that allowed the PLRA to take shape.[134] Specifically, the PLRA's consistency with the legislative process required by the Constitution, effect on the contours of the Bill of Rights, implications for prison reform, and utility as a rubric for adjudication all merit closer scrutiny.[135] The results of this scrutiny, coupled with an understanding of the mechanics of the PLRA, provide a cautionary tale for those intent on future reform.[136]

The PLRA as Legislative Subterfuge

To claim that the PRLA was passed "with strong bipartisan support and the support of the Clinton Administration" is something of a half-truth.[137] Because the PLRA was passed as an appropriations bill rider, it might not have received the same "strong bipartisan support" had it been submitted for legislative and executive review as a standalone bill?[138] On the contrary, the PLRA's passage was more a function of fiscal exigency than of sound policy.[139] The appropriations bill in whose "fine print" the PLRA was buried was enacted by a desperate Congress after months of budgetary crisis, and the PLRA's sparse legislative history attests to the cursory review it received amid the clangor.[140]

The difficulty with inserting provisions like the PLRA into omnibus appropriations bills is that they circumvent the deliberative process required by Article I of the Constitution.[141] Such provisions often escape legislators' attention, and the result is policy that runs contrary to the intent of Congress and the interests of the people.[142] And just as legislators are hard-pressed to give full consideration to individual provisions in a sweeping appropriations bill, the President has neither the time nor the constitutional authority to review and excise individual provisions from an omnibus budget bill.[143] Thus, a primary criticism of the PLRA is not that it is *bad* law, but that it is *not* law in the truest sense.[144] Legislation-by-misdirection may meet the technical requirements of bicameralism and presentment, but such formalism undermines the spirit of the Constitution and, in the case of the PLRA, facilitates violation of prisoners' Eighth Amendment rights.[145]

In addition to straining the precepts of the legislative process, the PLRA also reduces the Eighth Amendment from a steadfast prohibition to a mere advisory dictum with a generous "margin for toleration."[146] By limiting the circumstances in which the Eighth Amendment may be enforced, the PLRA encourages prisons to "[o]perate on the [m]argins of [c]ruelty."[147] The PLRA thus functions as something of a self-fulfilling prophecy: the Act is suffused with the language of limitation, and prison administrators, secure in the knowledge of these limitations, have a reduced incentive to fulfill what would otherwise be a constitutional duty.[148]

The PLRA also strains the Equal Protection provisions of the Fifth and Fourteenth Amendments because it creates "a separate but unequal system of access to courts that applies only to prisoners."[149] If the protections of these Amendments are as absolute as their language suggests, then the PLRA's limitation of them based on one's status as a criminal is inherently unconstitutional.[150] Moreover, the application of the PLRA to pretrial detainees who retain the presumption of innocence and to juvenile detainees who are deemed civil offenders rather than criminals curtails constitutional rights beyond even the PLRA's own justifications.[151] To the extent that the PLRA restricts these rights outside of the Article V amendment process, its legality is questionable.[152]

As the district court in *Plata* observed in a 2005 order, another principal flaw of the PLRA is its failure to comprehend substandard prison conditions as a "polycentric" issue.[153] In what appears to be an internal contradiction, the PLRA's "language invites scrutiny of proposed relief with a presumption against it."[154] That is, the PLRA highlights the many "subsidiary problem 'centers'" associated with prison overcrowding, but the "needs-narrowness-intrusiveness test," coupled with the requirement that courts give substantial weight to concerns for public safety and the criminal justice system, prohibits a polycentric solution.[155] Likewise, the PLRA's requirement that courts terminate relief orders upon compliance, even in the face of likely relapse, and the ability of prison administrators to move for termination of relief at specific junctures, regardless of compliance, militate against lasting reform.132 This counter remedial orientation impedes the courts in their role as a guarantor of prisoners' constitutional rights.[156]

Justice Scalia's dissent in *Plata* echoes a final criticism of the PLRA: that the Act's operative terms are pliable to the point of uselessness.[157] Where Justice Kennedy's majority opinion applied the "need-narrowness-intrusiveness" test to find that the prisoner release order was necessary, sufficiently narrowly tailored, and the least intrusive means of correcting the Eighth Amendment violations in California's prisons, Justices Scalia and Alito used the same statutory language to direct the opposite result.[158] For Justice Scalia, a statewide prisoner release order was neither narrowly drawn nor the least intrusive means of remedying the Eighth Amendment violations in specific prisons.[159] Similarly, Justice Alito found that the release order was premature because remedies short of a prisoner release could bring California's prisons into compliance with the Eighth Amendment.[160] Nor does the PLRA describe how to account for the "substantial weight" of the public safety analysis.[161] Justice Kennedy found that public safety concerns did not outweigh the need for a prisoner release, while Justices Scalia and Alito found that they did.[162] The lack of precise meaning in the PLRA's terms renders it little more than a flaccid judicial test that allows prisoners' constitutional rights to hang in the balance.[163]

LAW ON EXHAUSTION

The Prison Litigation Reform Act (PLRA) requires an inmate to exhaust prison grievance procedures before filing suit in federal court.[164] Exhaustion under PLRA is mandatory. *Jones, 549 U.S. at 211.* "[T]o properly exhaust administrative remedies, prisoners must 'complete the administrative review process in accordance with the applicable procedural rules,' rules that are defined not by the PLRA, but by the prison grievance process itself." *Id., 549 U.S. at 218* (quoting *Woodford v. Ngo, 548 U.S. 81, 88, 126 S. Ct. 2378, 165 L. Ed. 2d 368 (2006)).* Compliance with a prison's grievance procedures is, therefore, all that is required by the PLRA to properly exhaust. *Id.* Thus, the question of whether an inmate has properly exhausted administrative remedies will depend on the specifics of that particular prison's grievance policy. *See Id.* The prisoner must complete the administrative review process in accordance with the applicable rules.[165] Exhaustion is required for all suits about prison life,[166] regardless of the type of relief offered through the administrative process[167]. The defendant bears the initial burden to show that there was an available administrative remedy and that the prisoner did not exhaust it[168].

The defendant bears the ultimate burden of proving failure to exhaust.[169] If the defendant initially shows that (1) an available administrative remedy existed and (2) the prisoner failed to exhaust that remedy, then the burden of production shifts to the plaintiff to bring forth evidence "showing that there is something in his particular case that made the existing and generally available administrative remedies effectively unavailable to him." Albino, 747 F.3d at 1172. Confusing or contradictory information given to a prisoner is relevant to the question "of whether relief was, as a practical matter, 'available.'" Brown, 422 F.3d at 937. Administrative remedies will be deemed unavailable and exhaustion excused if the inmate had no way of knowing the prison's grievance procedure, if the prison improperly processed an inmate's grievance, if prison officials misinformed an inmate regarding grievance procedures, if the inmate "did not have access to the necessary grievance forms within the prison's time limits for filing the grievance," or if prison staff took any other similar actions that interfered with an inmate's efforts to exhaust. Albino, 747 F.3d at 1173. If a prisoner has failed to exhaust available administrative remedies, the appropriate remedy is dismissal without prejudice.[170]

"The point of the PLRA exhaustion requirement is to allow prison officials 'a fair opportunity' to address grievances on the merits, to correct prison errors that can and should be corrected and to create an administrative record for those disputes that eventually end up in court."[171] Thus, compliance with the PLRA requires that prisoners file a grievance against the person(s) they ultimately seek to sue.[172]

FOR PROFIT HEALTHCARE COMPANIES

ACLU[173] Lawsuit Charges Arizona Prison Officials with Failing to Provide Adequate Health Care, Inhumane Use of Solitary Confinement. Prisoners in the custody of the Arizona Department of Corrections receive such grossly inadequate medical, mental health and dental care that they are in grave danger of suffering serious and preventable injury, amputation, disfigurement and even death, according to a federal class-action lawsuit filed today by a legal team led by the American Civil Liberties Union and the Prison Law Office. The lawsuit also charges that thousands of prisoners are routinely subjected to solitary confinement in windowless cells behind solid steel doors, in conditions of extreme social isolation and sensory deprivation, leading to serious physical and psychological harm. Some prisoners in solitary receive no outdoor exercise for months or years on end, and some receive only two meals a day.

"The prison conditions in Arizona are among the worst I've ever seen," said Donald Specter, executive director of the Berkeley, Calif.-based Prison Law Office. "Prisoners have a constitutional right to receive adequate health care, and it is unconscionable for them to be left to suffer and die in the face of neglect and deliberate indifference."

"Courts have consistently ruled that solitary confinement of people with mental illness is unconstitutional because it aggravates their illness and prevents them from getting proper treatment," said David Fathi, director of the ACLU National Prison Project. "Even for those with no prior history of mental illness, solitary confinement can inflict extraordinary suffering and lead to catastrophic psychiatric deterioration."

Critically ill prisoners have begged prison officials for medical treatment, according to the lawsuit, only to be told to "be patient," that "it's all in your head," or that they should "pray" to be cured. Arizona prison officials have repeatedly been warned by their own medical staff of the inadequacy of the care, echoing complaints from prisoner advocates and families that prisoners face a substantial risk of serious harm and death. Yet, they have failed to ensure that minimally adequate health care is provided as required by the Constitution.

In one particularly tragic case, a prisoner at the state prison complex in Tucson died last year of untreated lung cancer that spread to his liver, lymph nodes and other major organs before prison officials even bothered to send him to a hospital. The prisoner, Ferdinand Dix, filed repeated health needs requests and presented numerous symptoms associated with lung cancer. His liver was infested with tumors and swelled to four times its normal size, pressing on other internal organs and impeding his ability to eat. Prison medical staff responded by telling him to drink energy shakes. He died in February 2011, days after finally being sent to a hospital but only after his abdomen was distended to the size of that of a full-term pregnant woman. A photograph of Dix shortly before his death appears in the lawsuit.

Jackie Thomas, one of the lawsuit's named plaintiffs who is housed in solitary confinement at the state prison complex in Eyman, has suffered significant deterioration in his physical and mental health as a result of being held in isolation, where he has become suicidal and repeatedly harmed himself in other ways. Prison staff have failed to treat his mental illness, improperly starting and stopping psychotropic medications and repeatedly using ineffective medications that carry severe side effects. Last November, Thomas overdosed on medication but did not receive any medical care.

"Faced with such gross indifference on the part of prison officials to the needs of prisoners with mental illness in their care, it was essential we get involved," said Jennifer Alewelt, staff attorney with the Arizona Center for Disability Law, one of the plaintiffs in the lawsuit. "Prisoners with mental illness can be particularly vulnerable, and we must do everything we can to ensure their mental health needs are met while incarcerated."

Filed in the U.S. District Court for the District of Arizona against Charles Ryan, director of the Arizona Department of Corrections, and

Richard Pratt, the department's interim director of the division of health services, the lawsuit asks, among other things, that constitutionally adequate health care be made available to prisoners, that medications be distributed to patients in a timely manner, and that prisoners not be held in isolation in conditions of social isolation and sensory deprivation that put them at risk of harm. The lawsuit does not seek monetary damages.

"Arizona has used the absence of transparency to callously ignore the basic needs of persons entrusted to its care, at times with deadly results," said Daniel Pochoda, legal director of the ACLU of Arizona. "Absent court intervention the health and well-being of thousands of prisoners will continue to be sacrificed to economic expediency."

According to the U.S. Bureau of Justice Statistics, Arizona has the sixth-highest incarceration rate in the nation.

Though private healthcare providers are killing inmates public officials refuse to discontinue the practce. "The purpose[174] of this letter is notify you of a potential monetary sanction of ten thousand dollars ($10,000.00) to be imposed for non-compliance with the terms and conditions of the above referenced contract between Wexford Health Sources ("Wexford") and the Arizona Department of Corrections ("Department")."

"The circumstances are as follows:

On August 27, 2012, between approximately 0600 and 0630 hours, while conducting diabetic insulin line in the medical unit at ASPC - Lewis - Morey Unit, Licensed Practical Nurse (LPN) N. Nwaohia contaminated a vial of insulin being used on the line. This contamination occurred when LPN Nwaohia drew insulin with a syringe for a Hepatitis-C positive inmate from a vial of "Regular" insulin and injected this insulin into the inmate. Utilizing the same syringe, she then drew a second dose of insulin from a vial of "Lantus" insulin and injected the secondary dose into the same inmate. LPN Nwaohia's actions contaminated the multi-dose "Lantus" vial. This vial was then utilized to provide insulin to other insulin dependent inmates.

Despite Wexford Nurse Lindsay Stephen becoming aware of this information on August 27, 2012, she did not file a report on the event until September 4, 2012. Rather, on August 27, 2012, she disposed of the insulin vials thought to have been involved in the contamination event and said nothing of the possible contamination event or her actions in destroying the insulin vials.

In speaking with Wexford Site Manager Sumi Erno on September 7, 2012, she reports contacting Wexford Regional leadership on August 28, 2012, specifically, Linda Maschner to report the incident to her. Ms. Erno. reported being directed by Ms. Maschner to begin identifying IDDM inmates so baseline testing of them for Hepatitis-C could commence. As a precaution, baseline testing was also conducted for HIV. (The index inmate, although known to be positive for Hepatitis-C, was subsequently tested for both Hepatitis-C and HIV.) Pending receipt of those test results, plans were implemented to test all inmates potentially exposed through this event for both Hepatitis-C and HIV. Test results for the index inmate later confirmed him as positive for Hepatitis-C and negative for HIV.

In identifying these inmates, Ms. Erno initially reported on August 28, 2012, as having 105 inmates at Lewis that receive insulin. This number later changed to 103, based on a spreadsheet created by Wexford medical personnel at the Lewis Complex listing inmates receiving insulin at Lewis. In review of this list duplication of some inmates was noted, thus the 103 number derived from this list was determined questionable.

Additionally, the Department received a report from Wexford generated from the online reporting system of their subcontracted Pharmacy (Diamond Pharmacy Service) on September 5, 2012, which reflected 91 inmates receiving insulin at Lewis. In an email coinciding with the provision of this report, Wexford Director Karen Mullenix, stipulates the report was generated by Wexford's Site Manager at Lewis (Sumi Erno) and that she (Mullenix) has concern with the information Ms. Erno has provided thus far.

Due to the continued fluctuation of information from Wexford regarding the number of potentially impacted inmates and the clear lack of systems in place to readily identify insulin dependent inmates/chronic care inmates, ADC deployed the following resources to ASPC-Lewis to support Wexford and ensure all possible data sources were culled to determine a true number of potentially affected inmates:

> On September 5, 2012 ADC deployed an Audit Nurse Supervisor and an Audit Nurse.
>
> On September 6, 2012, ADC deployed an Audit Nurse Supervisor, two Audit Nurses, a Pharmacy Monitor, Contract Monitor, and administrative support.
>
> On September 7, 2012, ADC deployed an Operations Director, an Audit Nurse Supervisor, Contract Monitor and administrative support.
>
> On September 6 and 7, 2012, ADC Health Service personnel and Wexford's Site Manager Sumi Erno and Director of Nursing Nicole Armenia reviewed inmate Medical

files/charts, Medical Administration Records and Diamond Pharmacy's ORP system; conducting comparative review of each to arrive at a comprehensive accounting of the total number of inmates thought to be on insulin. Upon conclusion of the review on September 6, 2012, the total number of inmates was determined to be 111.

On September 7, 2012, one additional insulin dependent inmate was identified who had not been previously identified increasing the total number to 112. This inmate was housed in the Inpatient Clinic which maintains its own/separate supply of insulin; thus this inmate would reportedly not have been affected by the cross contamination incident.

Of the 112 identified inmates, eight inmates were determined to not have received insulin on September 27, 2012, as they were being treated with medication that did not require injection. Additionally, seven inmates were determined to have been "no shows" for insulin line on August 27, 2012. Two showed for insulin line, but refused their insulin medication.

Based on this data, it was determined that 94 inmates were at risk from the contamination of the "Lantus" insulin vial.

Despite information to indicate that some inmates may not have been exposure candidates, such as the aforementioned that didn't show up for insulin line or refused insulin and/or where known carriers of Hepatitis C prior to the exposure event in conjunction with threat of HIV having been eliminated through HIV testing of inmate involved in the initial contamination event, it was determined during a teleconference with Jim Reinhart and Dan Conn on September 7, 2012 that all 112 identified inmates would be baseline tested. This was prudent, based on the noted lack of records management, specifically the inability to readily identify chronic care insulin dependent inmates and the inability to locate Medication Administration Records for five inmates appearing on the list.

Baseline testing occurred at ASPC - Lewis as follows:

August 29, 2012 -.. **1 Blood Draw**
August 30, 2012 - .... **40 Blood Draws**
August 31, 2012- ....**23 Blood Draws**
September 5, 2012 - ....**4 Blood Draws**
September 6, 2012 - ....**10 Blood Draws**
September 7, 2012 - ....**29 Blood Draws**

Total: 107 Blood Draws

Three inmates appearing on the list were transferred to Kingman before their blood could be drawn at Lewis and ADC made arrangements to have ASP - Kingman Medical complete blood draws on these inmates which were completed by September 10, 2012. ADC also made arrangement for these inmates to be provided information regarding the contamination event necessitating the testing through Kingman medical personnel.

One inmate at Lewis refused to have his blood drawn and one other inmate was released prior to testing. Nicole Armenta, Wexford Director of Nursing at Lewis reported she had telephoned the released inmate's home and left a message for the inmate to contact her to arrange testing. As of September 11, 2012 there had been no known direct contact via Wexford with this inmate. On September, 11, 2012, ADC initiated contact with this released inmate through the Community Correction Bureau. The offender's assigned Community

Corrections Officer conducted a site visit at the offender's home, during which the offender telephoned the ADC Contract Monitor at Lewis in the presence of his Community Corrections Officer. The offender informed the Monitor that he had not taken any insulin on August 27, 2012 prior to being released. The offender was offered testing in accordance with the exposure protocol, which he declined and signed a Refusal to Submit to Treatment form 1101-4 on September 17, 2012, which was countersigned by his assigned Community Corrections Officer as a witness. Upon completion of the aforementioned testing, 110 of the potentially affected inmates completed baseline testing, and accounting for the two refusals, all 112 identified inmates have either been tested or offered testing.

The aforementioned significant issues require corrective action. In accordance with the contract's Special Terms and Conditions, Section 2.19 Contract Monitoring General Requirements, paragraph 2.19.7, you have ten (10) calendar days to appeal in writing disputing a finding of non-compliance that results in either a cure notice or a decision to refer the matter to the Chief Procurement Officer for action."

"Several[175] events detailing significant issues of non-compliance are described below:

August 17, 2012, ASPC-Perryville/Lumley Unit

> On August 17, 2012, Wexford nursing personnel were distributing medication on Lumley Unit - Yard 24 to include "watch swallow" medications. In accordance with "watch swallow" protocols, certain medications in powder form require administration to be completed via "floating" the medication in a small cup of water, which the patient drinks. During this distribution of medication, Wexford nurses

depleted their stock of cups prior to completing medication distribution to the inmate population. Wexford nurses tailed to stop the medication line and retrieve additional plastic cups, as would have been appropriate. Rather than refilling the supply of cups, a Wexford nurse placed the powdered "watch swallow" medication in an inmate's hand, directing the inmate to lick the powdered medication from her own hand.

This improper administration of medication instigated disorderly behavior by the affected inmate, requiring a security response. The nurses' disregard for proper protocol in administering this inmate's medication and their disrespect for the inmate are significant non-compliance issues that require corrective action.

August 22, 2012, Medication Expiration Report (Statewide)

During the month of August 2012, ADC conducted random reviews of prescriptions, utilizing the Medication Expiration Report published by Wexford for July 1 - August 11, 2012. In completing this review, ADC learned that a significant number of inmates may not have been receiving their medications as prescribed due to expired prescription(s) and inappropriate renewals or refills. Approximately 8,358 prescriptions required review and potential renewal to ensure inmates received their required medications.

Wexford's lack of communication to its field supervisors regarding the necessary process for reviewing the Medication Expiration Report for renewal of medication, together with Wexford's delayed response and lack of urgency to correct the identified problem, contributed to this significant non-compliance issue. Specifically, during a meeting on August

22, 2012, between ADC's Monitoring Bureau leadership and Wexford Regional and Corporate personnel, it was apparent, based on statements from Wexford's Corporate Pharmacist, Denise Mervis, Pharm.D., that Wexford was aware of the expired medication issue, but had not taken adequate, if any, action to correct it. In this meeting, Dr. Mervis referred to the expired medication renewals as a critical issue.

When asked on August 22, 2012 what actions Wexford had undertaken to correct this problem, Wexford leadership advised that they intended to conduct an initial review of the July 1, 2012 - August 11, 2012 Medication Expiration Report beginning August 27, 2012. Wexford's decision to wait five days to begin reviewing the Medication Expiration Report was an inadequate response to a significant issue of grave concern to ADC. As a result of Wexford's delayed response, ADC deployed State resources on August 23, 2012 to ADC prison complexes statewide to review various data sources in an effort to identify inmates in need of medication renewal and to ensure that renewal actually occurred. Multiple ADC prison complexes also enhanced security vigilance by increasing the rate of security checks to 30-minute intervals on all inmates to ensure the well-being of the inmate population.

August 23, 2012, ASPC-Florence/Central Unit

On August 23, 2012, an inmate was found hanging from a sheet in his housing location. ADC staff removed the sheet, placed the inmate on a gurney, and arranged for air transport to an outside hospital. The inmate (MH-3) was last seen by an ADC psychiatrist provider on May 1, 2012. At that time, the provider prescribed lithium carbonate, a "watch swallow" medication used as a mood stabilizer, for 180 days. Medication Administration Records (MARs) showed this inmate received his medication in May, June, and July. On July 18, 2012, during a psychiatric follow-up, the inmate reported that the lithium carbonate had been helpful in stabilizing his mood. During ADC's investigation of this incident, ADC determined that this inmate had not received his psychotropic medication for the first 23 days of August 2012, as evidenced by the feet that no MAR had been generated. Failing to deliver psychotropic medication as prescribed is a significant, non-compliance issue.

August 27, 2012, ASPC-Lewis/Morey Unit

On August 27, 2012, between approximately 0600 and 0630 hours, while conducting diabetic insulin line in the medical unit at ASPC - Lewis - Morey Unit, Licensed Practical Nurse (LPN) N. Nwaohia contaminated a vial of insulin being used on the line. This contamination occurred when LPN Nwaohia drew insulin with a syringe for a Hepatitis-C positive inmate from a vial of "Regular" insulin and injected this insulin into the inmate. Utilizing the same syringe, she then drew a second dose of insulin from a vial of "Lantus" insulin and injected the secondary dose into the same inmate. LPN Nwaohia's actions contaminated the multi-dose "Lantus" vial. This vial was then utilized to provide insulin to other insulin dependent, inmates.

Despite Wexford's Nurse Lindsay Stephen becoming aware of this information on August 27, 2012, Ms. Stephen did not file an Incident Report on the event, in accordance with ADC policy, until September 4, 2012. Rather, on August 27, 2012, she disposed of the insulin vials thought to have been involved in the contamination event and failed to notify Wexford management or appropriate ADC staff of the contamination event or her actions in destroying the insulin vials.

Wexford Site Manager Sumi Erno reported contacting Wexford Regional Manager Linda Maschner on August 28, 2012, to report the incident to her. Ms, Erno reported being directed by Ms. Maschner to begin identifying Insulin Dependent Diabetes Mellitus (IDDM) inmates so that baseline testing for Hepatitis-C could commence. As a precaution, baseline testing was also conducted for HIV. (The index inmate, although known to be positive for Hepatitis-C, was subsequently tested for both Hepatitis-C and HIV.) Pending receipt of those test results, plans were implemented to test all inmates potentially exposed through this event for both Hepatitis-C and HIV. Test results for the index inmate later confirmed him as positive for Hepatitis-C and negative for HIV.

Also, on August 28, 2012, upon direction of Wexford Management, Wexford RN Supervisor Sienkiewicz contacted AB Staffing, the subcontracted employer of LPN Nwaohia. Ms. Sienkiewicz reportedly advised AB Staffing that LPN Nwaohia would be prohibited from performing nursing services in support of Wexford contracts in the state. Wexford requested that AB Staffing file a complaint with the Arizona State Board of Nursing regarding LPN Nwaohia's actions. One week later, on September 4, 2012, while following up at ADC's request, Wexford learned that no complaint regarding LPN Nwaohia had been received by the Board. Wexford Regional Manager Maschner then formally submitted the complaint on the afternoon of September 4, 2012.

In identifying IDDM inmates, Ms. Erno initially reported on August 28, 2012, as having 105 inmates at Lewis that receive insulin. This number later changed to 103, following review of a spreadsheet created by Wexford medical personnel at the Lewis Complex listing inmates receiving insulin at Lewis. In review of this list, duplication of some inmates was noted, thus the 103 number derived from this list was determined questionable.

Additionally, the Department received a report from Wexford generated from the online reporting system of their subcontracted Pharmacy (Diamond Pharmacy Service) on September 5, 2012, which reflected 91 inmates receiving insulin at Lewis. In an email coinciding with the provision of this report, Wexford Director Karen Mullenix, stipulated that the report was generated by Wexford's Site Manager at Lewis (Sumi Emo) and that she (Mullenix) had concerns with the validity of the information Ms. Erno had provided thus far.

On September 5, 2012, during a meeting with inmates at ASPC-Lewis, an additional 9 inmates not previously identified by Wexford were added to the list of those potentially exposed.

Due to the continued fluctuation of information from Wexford and the lack of systems in place to readily identify insulin dependent/chronic care inmates, ADC deployed additional compliance monitoring staff to ASPC-Lewis on September 5, 6, & 7. Wexford did not deploy additional resources to the site until September 6, 2012. It was not until Friday, September 7, 2012, that the total population of insulin dependent inmates and the subset of potentially exposed inmates were identified with certainty. Further, baseline testing of this population was not completed until September 10, 2012, despite Wexford's earlier reporting that this had been completed on September 4, 2012.

The failure to follow established nursing protocols, poor record keeping, mismanagement of documentation, inadequate and inaccurate communication, lack of timely managerial or administrative support, and failure to ensure that corrective action had been completed represent serious issues of non-compliance.

September 13, 2012, ASPC-Perryville/Santa Rosa Unit

On September 13, 2012, at approximately 1715 hours, Wexford Director Karen Mullenix notified ADC of a possible case of pertussis (whooping cough) at ASPC-Perryville. Wexford management did not know the name(s) or number(s) of inmate(s) affected, or the unit(s) identified with the reported case. Wexford's notification of the reported pertussis case was inadequate and inconsistent. Further, without sufficient factual detail of the incident, Wexford reported no action plan to address the situation.

Ms. Mullenix further reported that Wexford's Dr. Palmer spoke to both the County and State Health Departments about the case. She also reported that Dr. Bell (Regional Medical Manager) was called about this issue two days prior, September 11, 2012, and although he was aware of the potential diagnosis, that information had not been communicated to either Ms. Mullenix or the ADC Site Monitors. ADC Audit Nurse Mendoza contacted Wexford facility personnel and determined that an inmate tested positive for pertussis on August 13, 2012, approximately 30 days prior to Wexford's notification to ADC. ADC Audit Nurse Mendoza also confirmed the inmate's name, number and location.

In a phone conversation later that evening with Site Manager Deb Cherry and Richard Pratt, ADC Interim Assistant Director, Health Services Monitoring Bureau, it was reported that Dr. Palmer had seen the inmate who tested positive for pertussis approximately 10 days prior to Wexford's notification to ADC. Ms. Cherry also advised she was aware of this issue up to 10 days prior and failed to advise either Ms. Mullenix or ADC Site Monitors at that time. During ADC's investigation, Ms. Cherry speculated that the patient may have unknowingly contracted the disease through inmate visitation in the past few weeks, as the inmate was later contacted by her visitor to advise she or her child had been diagnosed with pertussis. Ms. Cherry also reported that Dr. Palmer contacted the County Health Department regarding the case and that she ordered 25 test kits from the Maricopa County Health Department to test any additional suspected cases of pertussis. That, in fact, was not the case. Ms. Cherry sent an "undeliverable" e-mail to the County's website, requesting the test kits.

A known case of a reportable infectious disease went unreported to ADC staff and Wexford State Level Management for 30 days, indicating a lack of urgency, a lack of awareness of the situation's potential seriousness, a breakdown of communication between field personnel and management, or all of the above. Further, Wexford's failure to independently engage in developing a plan by which to identify/confirm current and future suspected cases of pertussis is a significant non-compliance issue."

"Controller Chelsa Wagner[176] made the announcement at the jail oversight board meeting Thursday, nearly two weeks after county officials announced they will not renew the contract with the Tennessee-based firm that expires at the end of August. The agreement included three one-year options that could have moved it into 2018."

"I think we need to memorialize exactly where we are as Corizon is leaving," said the board's chairman, Common Pleas Judge Joseph Williams III, who requested the audit."

"County Executive Rich Fitzgerald announced May 22 that the county will bring the jail infirmary operation in-house, but he has yet to name what Judge Williams' called the "medical giants and universities" set to be involved. In May, the judge said Carnegie Mellon University, the University of Pittsburgh, UPMC and Allegheny Health Network "have agreed that they'll partner in different ways to help us get on track as to where we ought to be with respect to health care" at the jail.

"The Allegheny County[177] Jail's medical care provider has "ripped off" taxpayers and put the health of inmates and employees at risk, county Controller Chelsa Wagner"

"There's an issue of inmate health. There's an issue of employee health, and then there's an issue of the taxpayers' money," Wagner said. "It's very clear that the taxpayers are being ripped off. We're paying them for services that they are not providing."

"Wagner started her audit of Corizon in February, citing reports of substandard care, and examined the first six months of the contract. Corizon, a Tennessee-based health care giant, began offering care at the jail Sept. 1, 2013. It won a five-year contract that could cost the county more than $62.55 million."

"A Birmingham, Alabama health care company [178] has taken over medical care at the Washington County jail in Hillsboro, Oregon in the wake of a scathing audit that led county officials to terminate a contract with Corizon Health two years early. The audit found that a lack of county oversight of the Corizon contract resulted in inadequate prisoner medical care and cost the county hundreds of thousands of dollars."

"Birmingham-based NaphCare, Inc. assumed control over health care at the jail on June 1, 2015 under a contract to provide services to the approximately 570 prisoners at the facility."

"We are eager to embark on this partnership with NaphCare. They are an organization that shares our commitment to value-driven service while providing progressive medical care within our jail," Sheriff Pat Garrett said in a statement.

"Recent news for for-profit prison and jail healthcare provider Corizon[179] with respect to contract renewals has not been good. In June 2015, it was announced that two of the company's clients, the New York City jail system – including Rikers Island – and the Allegheny County Jail in Pennsylvania, would not be renewing their contracts with Corizon to provide medical services to prisoners. In both cases, the contracts were not renewed due to issues related to the company's performance."

"On June 10, 2015, New York City Mayor Bill de Blasio announced he would not renew Corizon's contract to provide healthcare at Rikers Island and other city jails; the $126.6 million contract is set to expire on December 31, 2015. According to *DNAinfo New York*, the company's contracts are actually worth over $400 million. Corizon was awarded a $126.6 million contract for management of medical services in the city's jail system. The city also awarded Correctional

Medical Associates of NY (CMA of NY) a $270 million contract to provide health care to jail prisoners, and awarded Correctional Dental Associates of NY (CDA of NY) $8.98 million to provide dental care. CMA of NY has the same corporate address as Brentwood, Tennessee-based Corizon, and prior to 2012, CDA of NY was registered as PHS Dental Services, Inc. PHS, or Prison Health Services, was a predecessor to Corizon. [See: *PLN,* July 2015, p.1]."

"Following eleven deaths within an 18-month period at the Allegheny County Jail in Pittsburgh, Pennsylvania, county executive Rich Fitzgerald announced that the jail's contract with Corizon would not be renewed after expiring at the end of August 2015."

"In September 2013, Corizon was awarded a two-year, $23 million contract to provide health care services to prisoners at the Allegheny County Jail. However, problems with the company's performance began almost immediately. A prisoner jumped from a tier at the jail in October 2013 and was severely injured; he was not transported to the hospital until the following day. Within hours of his transfer, he died at the hospital from injuries sustained in the fall. Early on in the contract there were problems related to the proper and timely distribution of medication to prisoners, lack of adequate recordkeeping procedures, and staffing cuts that resulted in fewer registered nurses, physicians and mental health care personnel."

"At the El Paso County Jail in Texas, Corizon had held the contract for health care services since 2009. However, county officials began negotiations with the University of Texas Health System and the Emergence Health Network of El Paso to provide prisoner medical and mental health services at the facility. Corizon's contract expired and the company was granted a six-month extension until December 31, 2015 to continue to provide medical care for prisoners. The expired contract was worth approximately $8 million per year."

"In Santa Barbara County, California, the county's contract with Corizon expired on June 30, 2015. Although jail officials wanted to renew the contract, county commissioners granted only a 4-month extension, putting the $9.8 million annual contract on hold. At issue was deaths of prisoners at the facility, complaints of understaffing and medication shortages".

"Another civil lawsuit[180] against the contractor hired to handle all the healthcare needs of inmates at the Chatham County Jail has been filed in Savannah.This time it involves a non-violent inmate who claims negligence on the part of Corizon Health nurses at the jail, leaving him with permanent injuries."

"The prison healthcare market has flourished as state Departments of Corrections and local governments seek ways to save money and reduce exposure to litigation. [See: PLN, May 2012, p.22]. Only a few major companies dominate the industry. Corizon's competitors include Wexford Health Sources, Armor Correctional Health Services, NaphCare, Correct Care Solutions and Centurion Managed Care – the latter being a joint venture of MHM Services and Centene Corporation. Around 20 states outsource all or some of the medical services in their prison systems."

"As Corizon is privately held, there is little transparency with respect to its internal operations and financial information, including costs of litigation when prisoners (or their surviving family members) sue the company, often alleging inadequate medical care. For example, when Corizon was questioned by the news media in Florida during a contract renewal, the company initially tried to prevent the release of its litigation history, claiming it was a "trade secret."

Following a competitive bidding process, Corizon was selected to continue providing medical care to Indiana state prisoners under a three-year contract effective January 1, 2014. The contract has a cap of $293 million, based on a per diem fee of $9.41 per prisoner. Three weeks later, a lawsuit filed in federal court named Corizon and the Indiana Department of Correction as defendants in connection with the wrongful death of prisoner Rachel Wood. Wood, 26, a first-time drug offender, died in April 2012; the suit, filed on behalf of her family, claims she was transferred from prison to prison and denied care for her serious medical conditions, which included lupus and a blood clotting disorder.

In an October 2013 Bangor Daily News article, Steve Lewicki, coordinator of the Maine Prisoner Advocacy Coalition, discussed the state of healthcare in Maine's prison system. "Complaints by prisoners are less," he said, noting that while medical services provided to prisoners are better than in the past, there are still concerns. This relative improvement coincided with the end of the state's contract with Corizon. The contract, valued at approximately $19.5 million, was awarded to another company in 2012. A year earlier, the Maine legislature's Office of Program Evaluation and Government Accountability (OPEGA) completed a review of medical services in state prisons. The agency contracted with an independent consultant, MGT of America, to conduct most of the fieldwork, and the review included services provided under Corizon's predecessor company, CMS.

The OPEGA report, issued in November 2011, cited various deficiencies in medical care at Maine prisons – including medications not always being properly administered and recorded by CMS staff. Although the company was notified of the problem, no corrective action was taken. CMS employees did not follow policies related to medical intake and medical records; OPEGA reported that 38% of prisoners' medical files had inadequate or inaccurate documentation regarding annual physical assessments, and that files were not complete or consistently maintained. The report found 11% of sick calls reviewed were either not resolved timely or had no documented resolution. OPEGA also criticized CMS for inadequate staff training.

At a January 2012 legislative committee hearing, state Senator Roger Katz asked Corizon regional vice president Larry Amberger, "My question to you is in light of this history, why should the state seriously be considering any proposal your company might make to get this contract back again?"

In response, Amberger criticized the methodology used by MGT during the assessment and said he believed Corizon provided quality medical care. Questioning and challenging the findings of an independent reviewer is the same tactic the company used in Idaho. Regardless, Corizon's contract to provide medical care to Maine state prisoners is now a part of history.

In the wake of seven[181] prisoner deaths and subsequent lawsuits, prison healthcare provider Corizon has decided to not seek renewal of its contract at Kentucky's Metro Corrections in Louisville.

For much of the last two decades, Corizon has been Metro Corrections' provider of prisoner healthcare. Its decision to walk away from its $5.5 million annual contract comes on the heels of the deaths of seven sick prisoners in the last year.

Three lawsuits have been filed in recent months, contending Corizon staff ignored or dismissed prisoners' complaints and doctors were slow to review the prisoners' conditions or to send them to a hospital.

A lawsuit filed in August on behalf of the family of Samantha George alleges that when she was taken to Metro Corrections on a charge of buying a stolen computer, she informed a nurse that she was a severe diabetic, needed insulin, and was feverish and in pain from a MRSA infection. She was so ill she was unable to keep water down.

The nurse contacted Corizon's on-call doctor to suggest George be sent to a hospital. To avoid that expense, the doctor said he would see George the next day. He never followed up on the matter.

George's mother, Theresa, called Metro Corrections to advise them of the serious of her daughter's condition, which required insulin hourly. "They said 'I'm looking at her right now and she's fine,'" said Theresa George. "Four hours later, she was dead.

Samantha George was found unresponsive in her cell on August 8, 2012, and was pronounced dead after being taken to a local hospital. It was concluded that she died of complications from a severe form of diabetes, compounded by heart disease.

Weeks after George's death, prisoner Kenneth Cross died at Metro Corrections. He was arrested after a traffic stop that occurred while a friend was taking him to a hospital for an overdose. The arresting officers believed Cross was faking the overdose, so they took him to Metro Corrections on a warrant for a drug possession charge.

The booking nurse noted Cross had "slurred speech" and fell asleep "several times during his interview." He was placed in a cell, where he was found unconscious hours later. A short time later he was pronounced dead; a medical examiner noted the cause of death as a drug overdose.

"Nodding off... clearly should raise a red flag in the case of someone who was arrested for drug possession," said Cross family attorney Gregory Belzley. "Either hospitalize him or put him under very careful observation in which he was not allowed to go to sleep."

The Cross case is similar to the April 2012 death of Savannah Sparks, 27, She died from opiate abuse and withdrawal only six days after entering Metro Corrections.

A December 2012 email from Metro Corrections Director Mark Belton advised his staff, "Mistakes were made by Corizon personnel and their corporation has acknowledged such mistakes." Six Corizon employees resigned amid an investigation into the deaths. With Corizon being out of its contract, a new contract will be selected amongst six proposed bidders.

LAWSUITS ON HEALTHCARE

"Fundamental failures that led to Mr. Harrison's unnecessary death. Corizon agreed to implement major changes in how it staffs jails throughout the entire state as a part of this settlement. The lawsuit revealed that Corizon allows uncredentialed Licensed Vocational Nurses to do the intake medical assessments only Registered Nurses are allowed to do under California law. When Mr. Harrison was arrested and taken to jail, he told the Corizon LVN that he drinks every day, his last drink was that day, and he has a history of alcohol withdrawal. The LVN decided not to provide Mr. Harrison with life-saving alcohol withdrawal protocols, and she sent him to the general jail population with no medical follow-up. Three days later, Mr. Harrison went into severe alcohol withdrawal -- Delirium Tremens – was having hallucinations, and was Tased and beaten to death by deputies. One of the family's attorneys, Michael Haddad, said, "After jail deputies beat and Tased their father to death, Martin Harrison's children beat them in court to win the largest wrongful death settlement in a civil rights case in California history." Haddad also said, "It was very important for us to stop Corizon from endangering jail inmates by staffing California jails with unqualified nurses." Haddad's partner, Julia Sherwin, said, "This settlement is going to change the business of correctional medicine around the country. If California inmates are entitled to have Registered Nurses -- and not unqualified LVN's -- do the work of RN's then so are inmates in Arizona, Florida, Alabama, New York, Michigan, and every other state where Corizon has contracts." Sherwin also said, "Corizon failed Martin Harrison. His legacy is to make sure Corizon does not fail other people who suffer from serious health conditions like alcohol dependence. Martin's family was committed to making sure his death was not in vain, and they succeeded completely." After four years of litigation, Haddad & Sherwin were joined at trial by co-counsel, Rick Friedman, of Friedman - Rubin, from Bremerton, Washington."[182]

In a September 6, 2012 the Eleventh Circuit Court of Appeals affirmed a $1.2 million Florida jury verdict that found Corizon – when it was operating as PHS – had a policy or custom of refusing to send prisoners to hospitals. The Court of Appeals held it was reasonable for jurors to conclude that PHS had delayed medical treatment in order to save money.[183] The jury verdict resulted from a suit filed against Corizon by former prisoner Brett A. Fields, Jr. In July 2007, Fields was being held in the Lee County, Florida jail on two misdemeanor convictions. After notifying PHS staff for several weeks that an infection was not improving, even with antibiotics that had been prescribed, Fields was diagnosed with MRSA. PHS did not send him to a hospital despite escalating symptoms, including uncontrolled twitching, partial paralysis and his intestines protruding from his rectum. A subsequent MRI scan revealed that Fields had a severe spinal compression; he was left partly paralyzed due to inadequate medical care.

The Eleventh Circuit wrote that PHS "enforced its restrictive policy against sending prisoners to the hospital," and noted that a PHS nurse who treated Fields at the jail "testified that, at monthly nurses' meetings, medical supervisors 'yelled a lot about nurses sending inmates to hospitals.'" Further, PHS "instructed nurses to be sure that the inmate had an emergency because it cost money to send inmates to the hospital."

At trial, the jury found that PHS had a custom or policy of deliberate indifference that violated Fields' constitutional right to be free from cruel and unusual punishment. The jurors concluded that Fields had a serious medical need, PHS was deliberately indifferent to that serious medical need, and the company's actions proximately caused Fields' injuries. The jury awarded him $700,000 in compensatory damages and $500,000 in punitive damages. [See: PLN, March 2013, p.54; Aug. 2011, p.24].

In February 2009, Frazier was incarcerated at the Manatee County Jail; at the time of his medical intake screening, staff employed by Corizon, then operating as PHS, noted that his health was unremarkable. Frazier submitted a medical request form in July 2009, complaining of severe pain in his left shoulder and arm, and a PHS nurse gave him Tylenol.

Throughout August and September 2009, Frazier submitted five more medical requests seeking treatment for his arm and shoulder. "It really hurts! HELP!" he wrote in one of the requests. PHS employees saw him and recorded his vital signs. Despite the repeated complaints, Frazier was never referred to a doctor or physician assistant; on September 9, 2009 his treatment was documented as routine but he was placed on the "MD's list."

In July 2011, after new complaints were filed regarding medical care at Idaho State Correctional Institution (ISCI) U.S District Court Judge B. Lynn Winmill appointed a special master, Dr. Marc F. Stern, to assess the situation at the facility. The court wanted Stern to confirm whether ISCI was in compliance with the temporary agreements established in the Balla case, and to investigate and report on "the constitutionality of healthcare" at the facility.

Dr. Stern, a former health services director for the Washington Department of Corrections who also had previously worked for CMS, one of Corizon's predecessor companies, issued a scathing report in February 2012. With the aid of psychiatrist Dr. Amanda Ruiz, Stern and his team reviewed ISCI over a six-day period and met with dozens of prisoners, administrators and Corizon employees.

Stern stated in the report's executive summary: "I found serious problems with the delivery of medical and mental health care. Many of these problems have either resulted or risk resulting in serious harm to prisoners at ISCI. In multiple ways, these conditions violate the rights of prisoners at ISCI to be protected from cruel and unusual punishment. Since many of these problems are frequent, pervasive, long-standing, and authorities are or should have been aware of them, it is my opinion that authorities are deliberately indifferent to the serious health care needs of their charges."

The report found that prisoners who were terminally ill or in long-term care were sometimes left in soiled linens, given inadequate pain medication and went for long periods without food or water. The findings regarding sick call noted instances in which prisoners' requests either resulted in no care, delayed care or treatment that was deemed dangerous. Emergency care situations had insufficient oversight, delays or no response; inadequately trained medical staff operated independently during emergencies without oversight from an RN or physician. The report also found problems with the pharmacy and medication distribution at ISCI.

In one case, a prisoner with a "history of heart disease was inexplicably dropped from the rolls of the heart disease Chronic Care Clinic." As a result, medical staff stopped conducting regular check-ups and assessments related to the prisoner's heart condition. A few years later the prisoner went in for a routine visit, complaining of occasional chest pain. No evaluation or treatment was ordered and the prisoner died four days later due to a heart attack. In another case, Corizon staff failed to notify a prisoner for seven months that an X-ray indicated he might have cancer.

Dr. Stern's report not only reviewed processes but also staff competency and adequacy. The report cited allegations that a dialysis nurse at ISCI overtly did not like prisoners, and routinely "failed to provide food and water to patients during dialysis, prematurely aborted dialysis sessions or simply did not provide them [dialysis] at all and failed to provide ordered medications resulting in patients becoming anemic." Stern concluded that prison officials were aware of this issue and the danger it presented to prisoners, but "unduly delayed taking action."

The mental health care provided by Corizon at ISCI was found to be deficient by Dr. Ruiz, who conducted the psychiatric portion of the court-ordered review. The report noted that the facility had 1) inadequate "screening of and evaluating prisoners to identify those in need of mental health care," 2) "significant deficiencies in the treatment program at ISCI" which was "violative of patients' constitutional right to health care," 3) an "insufficient number of psychiatric practitioners at ISCI," 4) incomplete or inaccurate treatment records, 5) problems with psychotropic medications, which were prescribed with no face-to-face visits or follow-up visits with prisoners and 6) inadequate suicide prevention training.

The report concluded: "The state of guiding documents, the inmate grievance system, death reviews and a mental health CQI [continuous quality improvement] system at ISCI is poor. While not in and of themselves unconstitutional, it is important for the court to be aware of this and its possible contribution to other unconstitutional events."

VICTIMS TARGETED BY HEALTHCARE PROVIDERS

To prevent victims of healthcare providers from filing suits and complaints they have engaged in retaliatory conduct and one court stated: "Plaintiff Shirley Jenkins[184], as Personal Representative for the Estate of Jovon Frazier, deceased, brought this section 1983 case against Defendant Corizon Health, Inc., alleging Corizon was deliberately indifferent to Frazier's serious medical needs because Corizon should have referred Frazier to an outside healthcare provider sooner. Specifically, Plaintiff alleged that, by the time Corizon referred Frazier to outside care, it was too late to avoid amputation of his left arm and his subsequent death due to osteosarcoma. And that it was Corizon's custom, policy, and practice to discourage diagnostic testing and outside care for financial reasons.

On March 24, 2016, the Court granted Corizon's dispositive motion for summary judgment (Dkt. 108) and on March 25, 2016, final judgment was entered in its favor (Dkt. 109).

Corizon now argues that it is entitled to attorneys' fees and costs because Plaintiff's section 1983 claim was frivolous, unreasonable, or without foundation. In response, Plaintiff argues that a failure to prevail on the claim does not render the claim frivolous or groundless, and that the Court carefully considered Plaintiff's claim prior to rendering judgment in Corizon's favor. Upon careful consideration of the parties' arguments, the Court declines to award attorneys' fees to Corizon.

In *Sullivan v. School Board of Pinellas County,* 773 F.2d 1182 (11th Cir. 1985), the Eleventh Circuit stated that "a district court may in its discretion award attorneys' fees to a prevailing defendant in a . . . section 1983 action upon a finding that the plaintiff's lawsuit was frivolous, unreasonable, or without foundation." *Id.* at 1188 (internal quotations omitted). "In determining whether a suit is frivolous, 'a district court must focus on the question whether the case is so lacking in arguable merit as to be groundless or without foundation rather than whether the claim was ultimately successful.'" *Id.* at 1189 (quoting *Jones v. Texas Tech University,* 656 F.2d 1137, 1145 (5th Cir. 1981)); *see also Christianburg Garment Co. v. EEOC,* 434 U.S. 412, 421 (1978);*Hughes v. Rowe,* 449 U.S. 5, 14 (1980).

The Supreme Court in *Christianburg* cautioned, as follows:

[i]n applying these criteria, it is important that a district court resist the understandable temptation to engage in post hoc reasoning by concluding that, because a plaintiff did not ultimately prevail, his action must have been unreasonable or without foundation. This kind of hindsight logic could discourage all but the most airtight claims . . . Even when the law or the facts appear questionable or unfavorable at the outset, a party may have an entirely reasonable ground for bringing suit. 434 U.S. at 421-22.

Notably, even if a defendant prevails on summary judgment in a section 1983 suit for damages, an award of attorneys' fees is not appropriate if the case was difficult, or if the "plaintiff's claims [were] meritorious enough to receive careful attention and review." *Busby v. City of Orlando,* 931 F.2d 764, 787 (11th Cir. 1991); *see also Walker v. Nationsbank of Fla. N.A.,* 53 F.3d 1548, 1559 (11th Cir. 1995). In *Hughes,* the Supreme Court noted:

Even those allegations that were properly dismissed for failure to state a claim deserved and received the careful consideration of both the District Court and the Court of Appeals. Allegations that, upon careful examination, prove legally insufficient to require a trial are not, for that reason alone, groundless or without foundation as required by Christianburg.

449 U.S. at 15-16 (internal quotations omitted).

In this case, the Court denied Corizon's motion to dismiss and the parties engaged in discovery. Ultimately, Plaintiff's claim against Corizon failed because the Court determined on summary judgment that Plaintiff could not establish, as a matter of law, that Corizon had a policy or custom in place that was the moving force behind a constitutional violation. Admittedly, the Court stated in its Order that there was not "even a scintilla of evidence establishing, or even suggesting" a policy or custom. But this does not necessarily render Plaintiff's claim baseless. The history of this case reveals that Plaintiff's complaint was sufficiently "meritorious enough to receive careful attention and review." *Busby,* 931 F.2d at 787. Accordingly, Corizon's motion for attorneys' fees is denied.

Corizon also moves for costs in the amount of $13,520.56. Although Corizon is clearly entitled to costs under 28 U.S.C. § 1920, Corizon neglected to file a Bill of Costs and its motion does not otherwise explain the requested costs in any way (other than to attach Exhibit B, which is an itemization of the costs without any supporting documentation), or state that the costs were necessarily obtained for use in this case. Accordingly, the request for costs is denied without prejudice to Corizon to renew its request by filing an appropriate Bill of Costs. The Bill of Costs shall attach documentation in support of the requested costs."

ARIZONA CLASS ACTION LAW SUIT SETTLEMENT

Aentered into the following stipulation about healthcare. However past history has shown that it does not follow orders by courts and have done exactly just that.

Plaintiffs and Defendants (collectively, "the Parties") hereby stipulate as follows:

I. INTRODUCTION AND PROCEDURAL PROVISIONS

1. Plaintiffs are prisoners in the custody of the Arizona Department of Corrections ("ADC"), an agency of the State of Arizona, who are incarcerated at one of the state facilities located in the State of Arizona, and the Arizona Center for Disability Law ("ACDL").

2. Defendants are Charles Ryan, Director of ADC, and Richard Pratt, Interim Division Director, Division of Health Services of ADC. Both Defendants are sued in their official capacities.

3. The Court has certified this case as a class action. The class is defined as "All prisoners who are now, or will in the future be, subjected to the medical, mental health, and dental care policies and practices of the ADC." The subclass is defined as

"All prisoners who are now, or will in the future be, subjected by the ADC to isolation, defined as confinement in a cell for

22 hours or more each day or confinement in the following housing units: Eyman–SMU 1; Eyman–Browning Unit; Florence–Central Unit; Florence–Kasson Unit; or Perryville–Lumley Special Management Area."

4. The purpose of this Stipulation to settle the above captioned case. This Stipulation governs or applies to the 10 ADC complexes: Douglas, Eyman, Florence, Lewis, Perryville, Phoenix, Safford, Tucson, Winslow and Yuma. This Stipulation does not apply to occurrences or incidents that happen to class members while they do not reside at one of the 10 ADC complexes.

5. Defendants deny all the allegations in the Complaint filed in this case. This Stipulation does not constitute and shall not be construed or interpreted as an admission of any wrongdoing or liability by any party.

6. Attached to this Stipulation as Exhibit A is a list of definitions of terms used herein and in the performance measures used to evaluate compliance with the Stipulation.

II. SUBSTANTIVE PROVISIONS

A. Health Care.

7. Defendants shall request that the Arizona Legislature approve a budget to allow ADC and its contracted health services vendor to modify the health services contract to increase staffing of medical and mental health positions. This provision shall not be construed as an agreement by Plaintiffs that this

budgetary request is sufficient to comply with the terms of this Stipulation.

8. Defendants shall comply with the health care performance measures set forth in Exhibit B. Clinicians who exhibit a pattern and practice of substantially departing from the standard of care shall be subject to corrective action.

9. Measurement and reporting of performance measures: Compliance with the performance measures set forth in Exhibit B shall be measured and reported monthly at each of ADC's ten (10) complexes as follows.

   a. The performance measures analyzed to determine ADC substantial compliance with the health care provisions of this Stipulation shall be governed by ADC's MGAR format. Current MGAR performance compliance thresholds used to measure contract compliance by the contracted vendor shall be modified pursuant to a contract amendment to reflect the compliance measures and definitions set forth in Exhibit B.

   b. The parties shall agree on a protocol to be used for each performance measure, attached as Exhibit C. If the parties cannot agree on a protocol, the matter shall be submitted for mediation or resolution by the District Court.

10. The measurement and reporting process for performance measures, as described in Paragraph 9, will determine (1) whether ADC has complied with particular performance measures at particular complexes, (2) whether the health care provisions of this Stipulation may terminate as to particular performance measures at particular complexes, as set forth in the following sub-paragraphs.

a. Determining substantial compliance with a particular performance measure at a particular facility: Compliance with a particular performance measure identified in Exhibit B at a particular complex shall be defined as follows:

i. For the first twelve months after the effective date of this Stipulation, meeting or exceeding a seventy-five percent (75%) threshold for the particular performance measure that applies to a specific complex, determined under the procedures set forth in Paragraph 9;

ii. For the second twelve months after the effective date of this Stipulation, meeting or exceeding an eighty percent (80%) threshold for the particular performance measure that applies to a specific complex, determined under the procedures set forth in Paragraph 9;

iii. After the first twenty four months after the effective date of this Stipulation, meeting or exceeding an eighty-five percent (85%) threshold for the particular performance measure that applies to a specific complex, determined under the procedures set forth in Paragraph 9.

b. Termination of the duty to measure and report on a particular performance measure: ADC's duty to measure and report on a particular performance measure, as described in Paragraph 9, terminates if:

i. The particular performance measure that applies to a specific complex is in compliance, as defined in sub-paragraph A of this Paragraph, for eighteen months out of a twenty-four month period; and

ii. The particular performance measure has not been out of compliance, as defined in sub-paragraph A of this Paragraph, for three or more consecutive months within the past 18- month period.

c. The duty to measure and report on any performance measure for a given complex shall continue for the life of this Stipulation unless terminated pursuant to sub-paragraph B of this Paragraph.

11. Defendants or their contracted vendor(s) will approve or deny all requests for specialty health care services using InterQual or another equivalent industry standard utilization management program. Any override of the recommendation must be documented in the prisoner's health care chart, including the reason for the override.

12. Defendants or their contracted vendor(s) will ensure that:

a. All prisoners will be offered an annual influenza vaccination.

b. All prisoners with chronic diseases will be offered the required immunizations as established by the Centers for Disease Control.

c. All prisoners ages 50 to 75 will be offered annual colorectal cancer screening.

d. All female prisoners age 50 and older will be offered a baseline mammogram screening at age 50, then every 24 months thereafter unless more frequent screening is clinically indicated.

13. Defendants or their contracted vendor(s) will implement a training program taught by Dr. Brian Hanstad, or another dentist if Dr. Hanstad is unavailable, to train dental assistants at ADC facilities about how to triage HNRs into routine or urgent care lines as appropriate and to train dentists to evaluate the accuracy and skill of dental assistants under their supervision.

14. For prisoners who are not fluent in English, language interpretation for healthcare encounters shall be provided by a qualified health care practitioner who is proficient in the prisoner's language, or by a language line interpretation service.

15. If a prisoner who is taking psychotropic medication suffers a heat intolerance reaction, all reasonably available steps will be taken to prevent heat injury or illness. If all other steps have failed to abate the heat intolerance reaction, the prisoner will be transferred to a housing area where the cell temperature does not exceed 85 degrees Fahrenheit.

16. Psychological autopsies shall be provided to the monitoring bureau within thirty (30) days of the prisoner's death and shall be finalized by the monitoring bureau within fourteen (14) days of receipt. When a toxicology report is required, the psychological autopsy shall be provided to the monitoring bureau within thirty (30) days of receipt of the medical examiner's report. Psychological autopsies and mortality reviews shall identify and refer deficiencies to appropriate

managers and supervisors including the CQI committee. If deficiencies are identified, corrective action will be taken.

B. Maximum Custody Prisoners.

17. Defendants shall request that the Arizona Legislature approve a budget to allow ADC to implement DI 326 for all eligible prisoners. This provision shall not be construed as an agreement by Plaintiffs that this budget request is sufficient to comply with the terms of this Stipulation.

18. Defendants shall comply with the maximum custody performance measures set forth in Exhibit D.

19. Measurement and reporting of performance measures: Compliance with the performance measures set forth in Exhibit D shall be measured and reported monthly as follows.

   a. The performance measures analyzed to determine ADC substantial compliance with the Maximum Custody provisions of this Stipulation shall be governed by the protocol used for each performance measure attached as Exhibit E. If the parties cannot agree on a protocol, the matter shall be submitted for mediation or resolution by the District Court.

20. The measurement and reporting process for performance measures, as described in Paragraph 19, will determine (1) whether ADC has complied with particular performance measures at particular units, (2) whether the Maximum Custody provisions of this Stipulation may terminate as to particular performance measures at particular units, as set forth in the following sub-paragraphs.

a. Determining substantial compliance with a particular performance measure at a particular unit: Compliance with a particular performance measure identified in Exhibit D at a particular unit shall be defined as follows:

i. For the first twelve months after the effective date of this Stipulation, meeting or exceeding a seventy-five percent (75%) threshold for the particular performance measure that applies to a specific unit, determined under the procedures set forth in Paragraph 19;

ii. For the second twelve months after the effective date of this Stipulation, meeting or exceeding an eighty percent (80%) threshold for the particular performance measure that applies to a specific unit, determined under the procedures set forth in Paragraph 19;

iii. After the first twenty four months after the effective date of this Stipulation, meeting or exceeding an eighty-five percent (85%) threshold for the particular performance measure that applies to a specific unit, determined under the procedures set forth in Paragraph 19.

b. Termination of the duty to measure and report on a particular performance measure: ADC's duty to measure and report on a particular performance measure, as described in Paragraph 19, terminates if:

i. The particular performance measure that applies to a specific unit is in compliance, as defined in subparagraph A of this Paragraph, for eighteen months out of a twenty-four month period; and

ii. The particular performance measure has not been out of compliance, as defined in sub-paragraph A of this Paragraph, for three or more consecutive months within the past eighteen month period.

c. The duty to measure and report on any performance measure for a given unit shall continue for the life of this Stipulation unless terminated pursuant to sub-paragraph B of this Paragraph.

21. Seriously Mentally Ill (SMI) prisoners are defined as those prisoners who have been determined to be seriously mentally ill according to the criteria set forth in the ADC SMI Determination Form (Form 1103-13, 12/19/12), which is attached hereto as Exhibit F and is incorporated by reference as if fully set forth herein. For purposes of this Stipulation, "intellectual disabilities," as defined by the current version of the Diagnostic and Statistical Manual of Mental Disorders (DSM), shall be added to the list of qualifying diagnoses on Form 1103.13. This definition shall govern this Stipulation notwithstanding any future modification of Form 1103.13 or ADC's definition of "Seriously Mentally Ill." All prisoners determined to be SMI in the community shall also be designated as SMI by ADC.

22. ADC maximum custody prisoners housed at Eyman-Browning, Eyman- SMU I, Florence Central, Florence-Kasson, and Perryville-Lumley Special Management Area (Yard 30) units, shall be offered out of cell time, incentives, programs and property consistent with DI 326 and the Step Program Matrix, but in no event shall be offered less than 6 hours per week of out-of-cell exercise. Defendants shall implement DI 326 and the Step Program Matrix for all eligible

prisoners and shall maintain them in their current form for the duration of this Stipulation. In the event that Defendants intend to modify DI 326 and the Step Program Matrix they shall provide Plaintiffs' counsel with thirty (30) days' notice. In the event that the parties do not agree on the proposed modifications, the dispute shall be submitted to Magistrate Judge David Duncan who shall determine whether the modifications effectuate the intent of the relevant provisions of the Stipulation.

23. Prisoners who are MH3 or higher shall not be housed in Florence Central- CB5 or CB7 unless the cell fronts are substantially modified to increase visibility.

24. All prisoners eligible for participation in DI 326 shall be offered at least 7.5 hours of out-of-cell time per week. All prisoners at Step II shall be offered at least 8.5 hours of out-of-cell time per week, and all prisoners at Step III shall be offered at least 9.5 hours of out-of-cell time per week. The out of cell time set forth in this paragraph is inclusive of the six hours of exercise time referenced in Paragraph 22. Defendants shall ensure that prisoners at Step II and Step III of DI 326 are participating in least one hour of out-of-cell group programming per week.

25. In addition to the out of cell time, incentives, programs and property offered pursuant to DI 326 and the Step Program Matrix for prisoners housed at maximum custody units specified in 24 above, ADC maximum custody prisoners designated as SMI pursuant to 21 above, shall be offered an additional ten hours of unstructured of out of cell time per week; an additional one hour of out-of-cell mental health programming per week; one hour of additional out of cell

pyschoeducational programming per week; and one hour of additional out of cell programming per week. Time spent out of cell for exercise, showers, medical care, classification hearings or visiting shall not count toward the additional ten hours of out of cell time per week specified in this Paragraph. All prisoners received in maximum custody will receive an evaluation for program placement within 72 hours of their transfer into maximum custody, including to properly identify all SMI prisoners.

26. If out of cell time offered pursuant to ¶24 or 25 above is limited or cancelled for legitimate operational or safety and security reasons such as an unexpected staffing shortage, inclement weather or facility emergency lockdown, Defendants shall make every reasonable effort to ensure that amount of out of cell time shall be made up for those prisoners who missed out of cell time. The out of cell time provided pursuant to paragraph 24 above, may be limited or canceled for an individual prisoner if the Warden, or his/her designee if the Warden is not available, certifies in writing that allowing that prisoner such out of cell time would pose a significant security risk. Such certification shall expire after thirty (30) days unless renewed in writing by the Warden or his/her designee.

27. Defendants shall maintain the following restrictions on the use of pepper spray and other chemical agents on any maximum custody prisoner classified as SMI, and in the following housing areas: Florence-CB-1 and CB-4; Florence-Kasson (Wings 1 and 2); Eyman-SMU I (BMU); Perryville-Lumley SMA; and Phoenix (Baker, Flamenco, and MTU).

a. Chemical agents shall be used only in case of imminent threat. An imminent threat is any situation or circumstance that jeopardizes the safety of persons or compromises the security of the institution, requiring immediate action to stop the threat. Some examples include, but are not limited to: an attempt to escape, on-going physical harm or active physical resistance. A decision to use chemical agents shall be based on more than passive resistance to placement in restraints or refusal to follow orders. If the inmate has not responded to staff for an extended period of time, and it appears that the inmate does not present an imminent physical threat, additional consideration and evaluation should occur before the use of chemical agents is authorized.

b. All controlled uses of force shall be preceded by a cool down period to allow the inmate an opportunity to comply with custody staff orders. The cool down period shall include clinical intervention (attempts to verbally counsel and persuade the inmate to voluntarily exit the area) by a mental health clinician, if the incident occurs on a weekday between 8:00 a.m. and 4:00 p.m. At all other times, a qualified health care professional (other than a LPN) shall provide such clinical intervention. This cool down period may include similar attempts by custody staff.

c. If it is determined the inmate does not have the ability to understand orders, chemical agents shall not be used without authorization from the Warden, or if the Warden is unavailable, the administrative duty officer.

d. If it is determined an inmate has the ability to understand orders but has difficulty complying due to mental health issues, or when a mental health clinician believes the inmate's mental health issues are such that the controlled use of force could lead to a substantial risk of decompensation, a mental health clinician shall propose reasonable strategies to employ in an effort to gain compliance, if the incident occurs on a weekday between 8:00 a.m. and 4:00 p.m. At all other times, a qualified health care professional (other than a LPN) shall propose such reasonable strategies.

e. The cool down period may also include use of other available resources/options such as dialogue via religious leaders, correctional counselors, correctional officers and other custody and non-custody staff that have established rapport with the inmate.

28. All maximum custody prisoners shall receive meals equivalent in caloric and nutritional content to the meals received by other ADC prisoners.

III. MONITORING AND ENFORCEMENT

29. Plaintiffs' counsel and their experts shall have reasonable access to the institutions, staff, contractors, prisoners and documents necessary to properly evaluate whether Defendants are complying with the performance measures and other provisions of this Stipulation. The parties shall cooperate so that plaintiffs' counsel has reasonable access to information reasonably necessary to perform their responsibilities required by this Stipulation without unduly burdening defendants. If the parties fail to agree, either party may submit the dispute for binding resolution by Magistrate Judge David Duncan. Defendants shall also provide, on a monthly basis during the pendency of the Stipulation, copies of a maximum of ten (10) individual Class Members' health

care records, and a maximum of five (5) individual Subclass Members' health care and institutional records, such records to be selected by Plaintiffs' counsel. The health care records shall include: treatment for a twelve (12) month period of time from the date the records are copied. Upon request, Defendants shall provide the health care records for the twelve months before those originally produced. In addition, Defendants shall provide to Plaintiffs on a monthly basis a copy of all health care records of Class Members who died during their confinement at any state operated facility (whether death takes place at the facility or at a medical facility following transfer), and all mortality reviews and psychological autopsies for such prisoners. The records provided shall include treatment for a twelve (12) month period prior to the death of the prisoner. Upon request, Defendants shall provide the health care records for the twelve months before those originally produced. The parties will meet and confer about the limit on the records that Plaintiffs can request once the ADC electronic medical records system is fully implemented.

30. In the event that counsel for Plaintiffs alleges that Defendants have failed to substantially comply in some significant respect with this Stipulation, Plaintiffs' counsel shall provide Defendants with a written statement describing the alleged non-compliance ("Notice of Substantial Non-Compliance"). Defendants shall provide a written statement responding to the Notice of Substantial Non-Compliance within thirty (30) calendar days from receipt of the Notice of Substantial Non-Compliance and, within thirty (30) calendar days of receipt of Defendants' written response, counsel for the parties shall

meet and confer in a good faith effort to resolve their dispute informally.

31. In the event that a Notice of Substantial Non-Compliance pursuant to 30 of this Stipulation cannot be resolved informally, counsel for the parties shall request that Magistrate Judge John Buttrick mediate the dispute. In the event that Magistrate Judge Buttrick is no longer available to mediate disputes in this case, the parties shall jointly request the assignment of another Magistrate Judge, or if the parties are unable to agree, the District Judge shall appoint a Magistrate Judge. If the dispute has not been resolved through mediation in conformity with this Stipulation within sixty (60) calendar days, either party may file a motion to enforce the Stipulation in the District Court.

32. Plaintiffs' counsel and their experts shall have the opportunity to conduct no more than twenty (20) tour days per year of ADC prison complexes. A "tour day" is any day on which one or more of plaintiffs' counsel and experts are present at a given complex. A tour day shall last no more than eight hours. No complex will be toured more than once per quarter. Tours shall be scheduled with at least two weeks' advance notice to defendants. Defendants shall make reasonable efforts to make available for brief interview ADC employees and any employees of any contractor that have direct or indirect duties related to the requirements of this Stipulation. The interviews shall not unreasonably interfere with the performance of their duties. Plaintiffs' counsel and their experts shall be able to have confidential, out-of-cell interviews with prisoners during these tours. Plaintiffs' counsel and their experts shall be able to review health and other records of class members, and records of mental health and other programming, during the

tours. Plaintiffs' counsel and their experts shall be able to review any documents that form the basis of the MGAR reports and be able to interview the ADC monitors who prepared those reports.

33. With the agreement of both parties, Plaintiffs may conduct confidential interviews with prisoners, and interviews of ADC employees or employees of ADC's contractors, by telephone.

34. Defendants shall notify the Ninth Circuit Court of Appeals of the settlement of this case and of their intention to withdraw the petition for rehearing en banc in case number 13-16396, upon final approval of the Stipulation by the District Court. Defendants agree not to file a petition for writ of certiorari with the United States Supreme Court seeking review of the Ninth Circuit's judgment in case number 13-16396.

IV. RESERVATION OF JURISDICTION

35. The parties consent to the reservation and exercise of jurisdiction by the District Court over all disputes between and among the parties arising out of this Stipulation. The parties agree that this Stipulation shall not be construed as a consent decree.

36. Based upon the entire record, the parties stipulate and jointly request that the Court find that this Stipulation satisfies the requirements of 18 U.S.C. § 3626(a)(1)(A) in that it is narrowly drawn, extends no further than necessary to correct the violation of the Federal right, and is the least intrusive means necessary to correct the violation of the Federal right of the Plaintiffs. In the event the Court finds that Defendants have not complied with the Stipulation, it shall in the first

instance require Defendants to submit a plan approved by the Court to remedy the deficiencies identified by the Court. In the event the Court subsequently determines that the Defendants' plan did not remedy the deficiencies, the Court shall retain the power to enforce this Stipulation through all remedies provided by law, except that the Court shall not have the authority to order Defendants to construct a new prison or to hire a specific number or type of staff unless Defendants propose to do so as part of a plan to remedy a failure to comply with any provision of this Stipulation. In determining the subsequent remedies the Court shall consider whether to require Defendants to submit a revised plan.

V. TERMINATION OF THE AGREEMENT.

37. To allow time for the remedial measures set forth in this Stipulation to be fully implemented, the parties shall not move to terminate this Stipulation for a period of four years from the date of its approval by the Court. Defendants shall not move to decertify the class for the duration of this Stipulation.

VI. MISCELLANEOUS PROVISIONS

38. Information produced pursuant to this Stipulation shall be governed by the Amended Protective Order (Doc. 454).

39. This Stipulation constitutes the entire agreement among the parties as to all claims raised by Plaintiffs in this action, and supersedes all prior agreements, representations, statements, promises, and understandings, whether oral or written, express or implied, with respect to this Stipulation. Each Party represents, warranties and covenants that it has the full legal

authority necessary to enter into this Stipulation and to perform the duties and obligations arising under this Stipulation.

40. This is an integrated agreement and may not be altered or modified, except by a writing signed by all representatives of all parties at the time of modification.

41. This Stipulation shall be binding on all successors, assignees, employees, agents, and all others working for or on behalf of Defendants and Plaintiffs.

PARTIAL PERFORMANCE MEASURES

ADOC agreed to the following performance measures as a part of the settlement and as is shown below, it is following these in the breach. This is because the Arizona Attorny General's saff in bad faith encourage breach of these stipulations and oders. It is not following these.

EXHIBIT A

For purposes of the performance measures, the following definitions will be used:

TERM DEFINITION

Active labor & delivery Contractions lasting 45-60 seconds and being 3 to 4 minutes apart ASPC Arizona State Prison Complex. ASPC-Safford includes Ft Grant. ASPC-Florence includes Globe. ASPC-Winslow includes Apache.

ATP Alternate Treatment Plan Chronic Disease Chronic diseases include the following:

    diabetes

    HIV/AIDs

    cancer

    hypertension

    Respiratory disease (for example, COPD / asthma / cystic fibrosis)

    Seizure Disorder

    heart disease

    sickle cell disease

    Hepatitis C

    Tuberculosis

    Neurological disorders (Parkinson's, multiple sclerosis, myasthenia gravis, etc.)

    Cocci (Valley Fever)

    End-Stage Liver Disease

    Hyperlipidemia

    Renal Diseases

    Blood Diseases (including those on anticoagulants (or long term >six months))

    Rheumatological Diseases (including lupus, rheumatoid arthritis)

    Hyperthyroidism

    Crohn's Disease

Contracted Vendor For purposes of this agreement, contracted vendor refers directly to Corizon Health and its subcontractors, or any successor contractor/subcontractor.

CQI Continuous Quality Improvement

Diagnostic Service Lab draws and specimen collections, X-rays, vision testing, and hearing testing

DOT Direct-observation therapy (watch-swallow) (medications)

Effective date of the Stipulation The date on which the Court grants final approval to the Stipulation.

Encounter Interaction between a patient and a qualified healthcare provider that involves a treatment and/or exchange of confidential information.

Healthcare staff Includes QHCPs as well as administrative and support staff (e.g. health record administrators, lab techs, nursing and medical assistants and clerical workers).

HNR Health Needs Request

HSCMB ADC's Health Services Compliance Monitoring Bureau

IPC Inpatient Component / Infirmary beds

IR Incident Report

KOP Keep-on-person (medications)

Licensed Healthcare staff who hold an active and unrestricted license in the State of Arizona in the relevant professional discipline.

MAR Medication Administration Record

Medical Provider Physician, Dentist, Nurse Practitioner, Physician's Assistant-C.

Any health care practitioner who has been duly empowered by the State of Arizona to write prescriptions.

Mental Health Clinician Psychologist, Psychology Associate

Mental Health Provider Psychiatrist, Psychiatry Nurse Practitioner

Mental Health Staff Includes QHCP's who have received instruction and supervision in identifying and interacting with individuals in

need of mental health services.

MH-1 (Mental Health 1)
Inmates who have no history of mental health issue or treatment

MH-2 (Mental Health 2)
Inmates who do not currently have mental health needs and are not currently in treatment but have had treatment in the past

MH-3 (Mental Health 3)
Inmates with Mental Health needs, who require current outpatient treatment. Inmates meeting this criterion will be divided into four (4) categories. These categories may change during each interaction with the inmate as their condition warrants.

MH-3A (Mental Health 3A)
Inmates in acute distress who may require substantial intervention in order to remain stable. Inmates classified as SMI in ADC and/or the community will remain a Category MH-3A (or MH-4 or MH-5 if in specialized mental health program).

MH-3B (Mental Health 3B)

Inmates who may need regular intervention but are generally stable and participate with psychiatric and psychological interventions.

MH-3C (Mental Health 3C)

Inmates who need infrequent intervention and have adequate coping skills to manage their mental illness effectively and independently. These inmates participate in psychiatric interventions only.

MH-3D (Mental Health 3D)

Inmates who have been recently taken off of psychotropic medications and require follow up to ensure stability over time.

MH-4 (Mental Health 4)

Inmates who are admitted to a specialized mental health program as identified in the Mental Health Technical Manual outside of inpatient treatment areas.

MH-5 (Mental Health 5)

Inmates with mental health needs who are admitted to an inpatient psychiatric treatment program (Baker Ward and Flamenco).

Prenatal screening tests GA/Preg, RPR, HIV, HEP, B & C, CBC, CMP (standardized lab panel), Urine, Rubella, ABO RH & Antibody

Psychology Associate A mental health clinician who has a master's or doctoral-level degree in a mental health discipline, but is not a licensed psychologist.

Qualified Health Care Professional (QHCP) Physicians, Physician Assistants, Dentists, nurses, nurse practitioners, dentists, mental health professionals, and others, who by virtue of their education, credentials/license, and experience are permitted by law to evaluate and care for patients.

Regular Business Hours Monday through Friday, 0800 am -1600 pm or similar 8-hour time frame; excluding weekends and holidays.

"Seeing a provider"/ seen/ "seen by"

Interaction between a patient and a Medical Provider, Mental Health Provider or Mental Health Clinician that involves a treatment and/or exchange of information in a confidential setting. With respect to Mental Health staff, means an encounter that takes place in a confidential setting outside the prisoner's cell, unless the prisoner refuses to exit his or her cell for the encounter

SMI According to a licensed mental health clinician or provider, possessing a qualifying mental health diagnosis as indicated on the SMI Determination Form (#1103.13) as well as a severe functional impairment directly relating to the mental illness.

All inmates determined to be SMI in the community shall also be designated as SMI in ADC. All inmates designated SMI (as defined in MHTM Chapter 2, Section 2.0) will be designated a MH-3A, MH-4, or MH-5 based on their current program placement.

SNO Special Needs Order

Specialized Medical Housing

Infirmary beds (IPC)

EXHIBIT B

HEALTH CARE OUTCOME MEASURES

Staffing 1 Each ASPC will maintain, at a minimum, one RN onsite 24/7, 7 days/week.

Staffing 2 Each ASPC will maintain, at a minimum, one Medical Provider (not to include a dentist) onsite during regular business hour and on-call at all other times.

Staffing 3 Dental staffing will be maintained at current contract levels –30 dentists.

Staffing 4 Infirmary staffing will be maintained with a minimum staffing level of 2 RNs on duty in the infirmary at all times at Tucson & Florence infirmaries and a minimum of one RN on duty in the infirmary at all times at Perryville and Lewis infirmaries

Medical Records 5 will be accurate, chronologically maintained, and scanned or filed in the patient's chart within two business days, with all documents filed in their designated location.

Medical Records 6 Provider orders will be noted daily with time, date, and name of person taking the orders off.

Medical Records 7 Medical record entries will be legible, and complete with time, name stamp and signature present.

Medical Records 8 Nursing protocols/NETS will be utilized by nurses for sick call.

Medical Records 9 SOAPE format will be utilized in the medical record for encounters.

Medical Records 10 Each patient's medical record will include an up-to-date Master Problem list.

Pharmacy 11 Newly prescribed provider-ordered formulary medications will be provided to the inmate within 2 business days after prescribed, or on the same day, if prescribed STAT.

Pharmacy 12 Medical record will contain documentation of refusals or "no shows."

Pharmacy 13 Chronic care and psychotropic medication renewals will be completed in a manner such that there is no interruption or lapse in medication.

Pharmacy 14 Any refill for a chronic care or psychotropic medication that is requested by a prisoner between three and seven business days prior to the prescription running out will be completed in a manner such that there is no interruption or lapse in medication.

Pharmacy 15 Inmates who refuse prescribed medication (or no show) will be counseled by a QHCP after three consecutive refusals.

Pharmacy 16 Perpetual inventory medication logs will be maintained on each yard.

Pharmacy 17 The Medication Administration Record (MAR) will reflect dose, frequency, start date and nurse's signature.

Pharmacy 18 Daily delivery manifests will be kept in binders located in medication rooms on each yard/complex and will be reviewed and initialed daily by an LPN or RN.

Pharmacy 19 Perpetual inventory medications will be signed off on the Inmate's individual MAR.

Pharmacy 20 Medical AIMs entries are accurately completed within 3 business days from the entry in the medical record.

Pharmacy 21 Inmates who are paroled or released from ASPCs will receive a 30-day supply of all medications currently prescribed by the ADC contracted vendor.

Pharmacy 22 Non-formulary requests are reviewed and approved, disapproved, or designated for an alternate treatment plan (ATP) within two business days of the prescriber's order.

Equipment 23 Automated External Defibrillators (AEDs) will be maintained and readily accessible to Health Care Staff. Equipment 24 Emergency medical response bags are checked daily, inventoried monthly, and contain all required essential items.

Emergency Response 25 A first responder trained in Basic Life Support responds and adequately provides care within three minutes of an emergency.

Quality Improvement 26 Responses to health care grievances will be completed within 15 working days of receipt (by health care staff) of the grievance.

Quality Improvement 27 Each ASPC facility will conduct monthly CQI meetings, in accordance with NCCHC Standard P-A-06

Quality Improvement 28 Every medical provider will undergo peer reviews annually with reviews and recommended actions documented.

Quality Improvement 29 Each ASPC facility Director of Nursing or designee will conduct and document annual clinical performance reviews of nursing staff as recommended by NCCHC standard P-C-02.

Quality Improvement 30 The initial mortality review of an inmate's death will be completed within 10 working days of death.

Quality Improvement 31 Mortality reviews will identify and refer deficiencies to appropriate managers and supervisors, including CQI committee, and corrective action will be taken.

Quality Improvement 32 A final independent clinical mortality review will be completed by the Health Services Contract Monitoring Bureau for all mortalities within 10 business days of receipt of the medical examiner's findings.

Intake facility 33 All inmates will receive a health screening by an LPN or RN within one day of arrival at the intake facility.

Intake facility 34 A physical examination including a history will be completed by a Medical Provider (not a dentist) by the end of the second full day of an intake inmate's arrival at the intake facility.

Intersystem Transfers 35 All inmate medications (KOP and DOT) will be transferred with and provided to the inmate or otherwise provided at the receiving prison without interruption.

Access to care 36 A LPN or RN will screen HNRs within 24 hours of receipt.

Access to care 37 Sick call inmates will be seen by an RN within 24 hours after an HNR is received (or immediately if identified with an emergent need, or on the same day if identified as having an urgent need).

Access to care 38 Vital signs, to include weight, will be checked and documented in the medical record each time an inmate is seen during sick call.

Access to care 39 Routine provider referrals will be addressed by a Medical Provider and referrals requiring a scheduled provider appointments will be seen within fourteen calendar days of the referral.

Access to care 40 Urgent provider referrals are seen by a Medical Provider within 24 hours of the referral.

Access to care 41 Emergent provider referrals are seen immediately by a Medical Provider.

Access to care 42 A follow-up sick call encounter will occur within the time frame specified by the Medical or Mental Health Provider.

Access to care 43 Inmates returning from an inpatient hospital stay or ER transport will be returned to the medical unit and be assessed by a RN or LPN on duty there.

Access to care 44 Inmates returning from an inpatient hospital stay or ER transport with discharge recommendations from the hospital shall have the hospital's treatment recommendations reviewed and acted upon by a medical provider within 24 hours.

Diagnostic Services 45 On-site diagnostic services will be provided the same day if ordered STAT or urgent, or within 14 calendar days if routine

Diagnostic Services 46 A Medical Provider will review the diagnostic report, including pathology reports, and act upon reports with abnormal values within five calendar days of receiving the report at the prison.

Diagnostic Services 47 A Medical Provider will communicate the results of the diagnostic study to the inmate upon request and within seven calendar days of the date of the request.

Specialty care 48 Documentation, including the reason(s) for the denial, of Utilization Management denials of requests for specialty services will be sent to the requesting Provider in writing within fourteen calendar days, and placed in the patient's medical record.

Specialty care 49 Patients for whom a provider's request for specialty services is denied are told of the denial by a Medical Provider at the patient's next scheduled appointment, no more than 30 days after the denial, and the Provider documents in the patient's medical record the Provider's follow-up to the denial.

Specialty care 50 Urgent specialty consultations and urgent specialty diagnostic services will be scheduled and completed within 30 calendar days of the consultation being requested by the provider.

Specialty care 51 Routine specialty consultations will be scheduled and completed within 60 calendar days of the consultation being requested by the provider.

Specialty care 52 Specialty consultation reports will be reviewed and acted on by a Provider within seven calendar days of receiving the report.

Chronic care 53 Treatment plans will be developed and documented in the medical record by a provider within 30 calendar days of identification that the inmate has a chronic disease.

Chronic care 54 Chronic disease inmates will be seen by the provider as specified in the inmate's treatment plan, no less than every 180 days unless the provider documents a reason why a longer time frame can be in place.

Chronic care 55 Disease management guidelines will be implemented for chronic diseases.

Chronic care 56 Inmates with a chronic disease will be provided education about their condition/disease which will be documented in the medical record.

THE MOTION TO ENFORCE THE SETTLEMENT

The State Of Arizona Department Of Corrections has a well-documented history in all matters, of entering into agreements and not complying with them. They consistently violate rights of prisoners with impunity and this is another instance. The motion to enforce provides in pertinent part as follows:

The Parsons Stipulation requires ADC to comply with a set of 103 health care performance measures. [Doc. 1185 8] These performance measures were designed to determine whether ADC was providing essential health care services to the plaintiff class. To fulfill the terms of the Stipulation, ADC must meet or exceed a 75% compliance score on each measure at each prison complex for the first year, 80% for the second year, and 85% thereafter. [*Id.* at 20]

After a full year of auditing compliance with these performance measures, evidence from ADC's own audits reveals a dismal failure to meet the terms of the Stipulation. Review of Defendants' own compliance data for many of the key performance measures related to patient care show that defendants have consistently delivered failing scores.

Defendant health care audits, though skewed in defendants' favor due to methodology errors for some performance measures, amply document defendants' failure to implement critical systemic changes to the medical and mental health care delivery systems.

Month after month, particularly at the larger institutions which house 80% of the prisoners, the audits reveal that patients are exposed to a substantial risk of serious harm because Defendants fail to provide timely medical and mental health appointments, fail to provide timely medications, fail to deliver ordered care and fail to adequately monitor mentally ill patients, including those on suicide watch. For critical performance measures, defendants have consistently failed to reach the 75% compliance benchmark for the Stipulation's first year and, without dramatic changes, have no hope of attaining the 80% benchmark currently required for compliance in year two. As a direct result of these well-documented systemic deficiencies, patients needlessly suffer serious injury, illness and, in some cases, death. Two examples illustrate the all too frequent result of ADC's grossly inadequate health care system. A 26 years old inmate hanged himself at Eyman-Browning Unit .He was diagnosed with bipolar disorder and was treated with Lithium, until the medication was discontinued due to side effects. Mental health staff did not consider any other medication to treat his illness, and did not perform an adequate suicide risk assessment, despite his history of suicide attempts and several other suicide risk factors.

On April 28, 2015, he submitted a Health Needs Request (HNR) saying "I want to get back on my lithium as soon as possible; I'm having serious mental issues." He was scheduled to be seen by mental health staff, but the appointment never happened. After his suicide, the ADC psychological autopsy noted that he had not been seen by mental health staff as required by policy. The ADC Mortality Review Committee concluded that he did not receive adequate mental health care; that his death was preventable; and that a "delay in access to care" was a contributing cause of his death. In the months prior to Mr. Suicide, Defendants failed to comply with Performance Measures 87 (a prisoner with Mr. classification must be seen by a mental health clinician no less than every 30 days) and 98 (mental health HNRs must be responded to within specific timeframes). [Declaration of Pablo Stewart, M.D., Exhibit A [Expert Report of Pablo Stewart, M.D.] ("Stewart Rep.") ¶50-58, filed concurrently herewith], a Yuma prisoner, died on at age 59, after low-level Nursing staff repeatedly ignored his desperate pleas for help, and did not seek the assistance of a medical doctor, even after open weeping lesions on Mr. Body were swarmed by flies. [Declaration of Todd R. Wilcox ("Wilcox Decl.") ¶41-43, filed concurrently herewith] Mr. had end-stage liver disease with complications including massive fluid retention, groin wounds, and sepsis. On March 6, 2015, he submitted an HNR stating "my legs were bleeding with open weeping wounds sticking to my prescription socks. I am in severe pain. I cannot wear my socks nor get them on. I am in pain." The nursing response to this sick call request indicates that it is a "duplicate from 3/3/15." However, there was no request dated 3/3/15 in his medical record. Mr. filed another HNR on March 17, 2015 for shortness of breath and painful abdomen. He was told he would see a nurse at an unspecified time, which apparently did not occur. Four days later, he filed an HNR for worsening fluid retention and shortness of breath. Again, he was told "duplicate same as 3/17, you are on nurse line." Mr. Condition deteriorated and his fluid retention worsened to the point that his skin split open and became infected. By March 31, 2015, Mr. Situation deteriorated to the point that he was being swarmed by flies, which he reported to nursing staff in a HNR. Instead of investigating why a patient with split skin oozing pus and serum had a swarm of flies on the injury, the nurse the next day instead decided that Mr. did not need to be seen. More than a week later, on April 9, 2015, he finally was sent to the hospital, where he died. The ADC Mortality Review determined there were multiple triage mistakes made by nurses that impeded and delayed care for Mr. Plaintiffs' experts, Drs. Wilcox and Stewart, agree that compliance with the performance measures required by the Stipulation is not possible with the existing staff.

[Stewart Rep. ¶17-25, 114; Wilcox Decl. ¶9-12, 29-35, 140] There are too many vacancies for existing positions, and there are too few allocated positions. Thus, as the two examples above show and ADC's own audits described below confirm, critical lapses of care occur too often, with harmful or fatal results.

PROCEDURAL HISTORY

In October 2014 the parties reached a settlement agreement, the "Stipulation," in the constitutional class action filed by fourteen Arizona Department of Corrections ("ADC") prisoners and the Arizona Center for Disability Law ("Plaintiffs"). The Court found the Stipulation to be "fair, adequate, and reasonable," and it went into effect on February 17, 2015. [Doc. 1458 at 1] Under the Stipulation, Defendants agreed to comply with 103 healthcare measures throughout ADC prison facilities and to allow Plaintiffs' counsel to monitor their implementation of these measures. [Doc. 1185 ¶8, 29] Class certification was granted, and the plaintiff class consists of approximately 36,000 prisoners at ADC's ten state prisons. *See Parsons v. Ryan*, 289 F.R.D. 513 (D.Ariz. 2013), *aff'd*, 754 F.3d 657 (9th Cir. 2014), *reh'g en banc denied*, 784 F.3d 571 (9th Cir. 2015); ADC contracts the provision of medical, mental health, and dental services to Corizon Health Service, Inc. ("Corizon"). Corizon is not a defendant in this matter because the duty to provide constitutionally adequate health care and constitutionally suitable conditions of confinement is a duty ADC cannot delegate. ADC is the responsible party regardless of who it hires to provide care. [*See* Doc. 175 at 9-10]

STATEMENT OF FACTS

Review of Defendants' own compliance data for many of the critical performance measures related to patient care show that Defendants have consistently delivered failing scores.

DEFENDANTS' AUDITS DOCUMENT A BROKEN SYSTEM

A. Access to Medical Care

1. Sick call

Patients in a prison facility must have an effective method for making their medical needs known to the medical staff. ADC prisoners seeking a medical appointment must submit a written health needs request form ("HNR"). Because these forms provide such a crucial link between medical staff and prisoners, Defendants' response time in triaging HNRs and then providing access to appropriate care is an essential monitoring parameter. Under the Stipulation and the CGAR audit, patients who submit sick call slips must be seen the same day for urgent needs; otherwise, they must be seen by nurses for sick call ("nurse line") within 24 hours of the triage. Based upon the nurse's assessment, the patient may or may not be referred and scheduled to see a primary care provider. Failure to adhere to these timelines places patients at serious risk of substantial harm. Dr. Wilcox, who reviewed the CGAR audit results in addition to medical records, concluded that Defendants' "sick call system remains profoundly deficient." [Wilcox Decl. 39] According to the CGAR reports, for the eleven month period of February through December 2015, *none* of the six largest ADC prisons achieved an average score of 75% or higher, and at Yuma, on average, just four in ten patients were seen timely during that period. As illustrated in the chart below, for the month of December, two large prisons, Eyman and Lewis, scored under 50%. [Wilcox Decl. 16] If the nurse determines the patient requires the attention of a primary care provider on a routine basis, the patient must be scheduled and seen by the provider within 14 days of the nurse appointment.9 Defendants' scores on this performance measure are likewise dismal. The CGAR results for the months of February through December demonstrate widespread non-compliance with the 14-day benchmark, particularly at the five largest men's prisons and at Perryville, the women's prison.10 At three of the five largest men's prisons, during the eleven months from February through December 2015, the average compliance rate for Measure 39 was below 75%, with Tucson scoring 50%. Perryville Scored at 48%. [Wilcox Decl. 46] The data underlying the CGAR reports document that patients who should be seen within two weeks may wait six weeks or more to see the provider. For example:

In November, some patients at Perryville were waiting six weeks to see a provider;

At Tucson's Winchester Unit, six of ten patients referred to the provider in October were not seen by the time of the November 26, 2015 audit; at Catalina Unit, five of ten patients referred in October were not seen by the time of the audit, and an additional patient had been seen but not in relation to the referral; at Santa Rita Unit, five of ten patients referred in October were not seen timely, and three were not seen at all;

At Florence, three of four East Unit patients referred in October were not seen as of the time of November 30, 2015 audit; at Kasson Unit, six of eight patients were not seen timely, and three were not seen at all;

At Eyman, six of six Browning Unit patients, three of six Meadows Unit patients, and three of five Cook Unit patients referred in October had not been seen at time of audit on November 30, 2015;

Tucson complex-wide compliance rate of 60% in December 2015; eleven patients not seen by the time of the January 30, 2016 audit, including one three month delay;

Yuma complex-wide compliance rate of 68% in December;

At Eyman, six of six Browning patients, three of six Meadows patients, and three of five Cook patients referred in October not seen at time of January 30, 2016 audit;

Douglas patient referred to provider on December 3, 2015 not seen as of time of January 29, 2016 audit;

Florence complex-wide compliance rate of 74% in December 2015; at North Unit, three of six patients referred in December not been seen at time of audit on January 28, 2016; and three of five South Unit patients referred in December not

Seen at time of audit;

Phoenix complex-wide compliance rate of 72% for December 2015; multiple prisoners referred to the provider in early to mid-December still had not been seen at time of audit on January 29, 2016. [Wilcox Decl. 47]

2. Chronic Care

Patients suffering from chronic illness require regular and coordinated health care. "Regularly scheduled appointments allow providers to track the progress of patients with chronic illnesses and ensure appropriate levels of treatment." [Wilcox Decl. 49] Failure to monitor chronic illness risks the condition or disease getting out of control, ultimately harming the patient.

Performance Measure 5411 requires Defendants to see chronic care patients at medically appropriate intervals. The CGAR reports show widespread and continued noncompliance with this measure. From February through December 2015, five of the largest men's facilities and Perryville Complex all averaged below 75% compliance, with Tucson and Florence barely over 50% compliance. [Wilcox Decl. 50] What these percentages do not reveal is that some of the delays in chronic care appointments lasted over a year, with one lasting two years. Patients with active cancer diagnoses have had gaps of 2 to 6 months between chronic care appointments. [Wilcox Decl. 51] The CGAR reports described numerous problems, including, but not limitedTo:

At Tucson's Santa Rita Unit, one patient had a two year lapse between chronic care appointments, and at least two lapsed for over a year; on Cimarron Unit, patient with diabetes lapsed for over a year; on Manzanita Unit, patient with active cancer, ordered to be seen monthly, not seen for four months;

Perryville complex-wide compliance rate of 64% for December 2015; at Lumley Unit, a woman with "active cancer . . . with plans for radiation therapy" for thyroid cancer not seen for eight months, and another Lumley patient with rheumatoid arthritis not seen for a chronic care appointment for 19 months after her diagnosis; patient at Santa Rosa Unit with blood disorders and anemia not seen for 14 months;

Douglas complex-wide compliance rate of 45% for December 2015;

Four of ten files reviewed at Florence North Unit showed delayed appointments, including 8-month gap in appointments for patient with thyroid disorder and hypertension; at Central, patients with 9 and 14 month gaps between appointments; another patient with seizure disorder, Hepatitis C, and asthma with no chronic care appointment between early March and mid-December 2015;

At Yuma's La Paz Unit, two patients with seizure conditions seen late;

Patients at Winslow complex seen six weeks and three months later than medically needed and previously ordered by the provider.[Wilcox Decl. 51]

These are profound lapses in treatment that imminently endanger the lives of some of the system's most vulnerable patients.

3. Inpatient Care

Many of ADC's sickest patients are housed in the prison infirmaries, where the ADC medical providers are required to see them every 72 hours. The average audit results for two of the three men's prisons with infirmary units over eleven months in 2015 show shockingly poor compliance for this critical measure—32% for Tucson and 19% for Florence. [Wilcox Decl. 67]

4. Medication Administration

For a prison health care system to achieve a successful system of medication administration it must be able to (1) provide prescribed medications to prisoners in a "timely, consistent manner"; (2) ensure prescribed medications are "renewed regularly and without interruption"; and (3) ensure that prisoners transferred between complexes experience no gaps in medication administration. [Wilcox Decl. ¶126-127]

Defendants' medication system fails to meet any of these thresholds and "practically guarantees that patients will have gaps in receiving their medications." [*Id.* 127] The audits show Defendants routinely fail to provide patients with new prescriptions timely, in compliance with Performance Measure 11.13 the average scores over three months off February through December, 2015 were below 75% at six of the ten

Prisons, including at all five of the largest men's prisons. The following chart highlights in yellow each month in 2015 where the prison's compliance level was less than 75.

B. Access to Mental Health Care

1. Inadequate access to care.

The Health Needs Request form (HNR) is the primary means by which ADC prisoner's access non-routine mental health services. To ensure that prisoners are able to have their mental health needs addressed in a timely fashion, defendants must monitor responses to HNRs, based upon the category of need. The Mental Health Technical Manual sets forth 5 specific timeframes for different categories of HNRs (e.g. Emergency, Urgent Medication, etc.).17

Defendants have unilaterally decided to monitor only one of these five categories:

Those raising "routine non-medication issues." This presents a risk of serious harm, since without monitoring, there is no way to know if emergency or urgent HNRs are being responded to in a timely fashion, or indeed at all. But even with this critical monitoring defect, Defendants are still noncompliant with this measure, with Eyman and Florence each showing nine consecutive months of noncompliance, and Lewis, Phoenix, Tucson, and 'Winslow each showing two or more consecutive fronts of non compliance.

2. Inadequate monitoring of psychotropic medications.

Patients taking psychotropic medication, or who have recently discontinued such medication, must be monitored by a psychiatrist. Performance Measure 81 requires that "MH-34 prisoners who are prescribed psychotropic medications shall be seen a minimum of every 90 days by a mental health provider."rs Dr. Stewart, Plaintiffß' psychiatric expert, found that "ADC is persistently noncompliant with PM 81 at multiple prisons." Both Lewis and Tucson, two of Defendants' largest complexes, reported consecutive months of non-compliance with this measure.

II. DEFENDANTS' BROKEN HEALTH CARE SYSTEM HARMS PATIENTS AND PLACES ALL PRISONERS AT SUBSTANTIAL RISK OF HARM

A. Systemic Failures Result in Treatment Delays and Denials Causing Suffering and Death

Defendants' own audits establish that their health care delivery systems fail to Provide reliable access to care. This failure has directly harmed many class members and has placed every prisoner at serious risk of substantial harm. Often denying and/or delaying access to medically necessary care has immediate, catastrophic, and permanent Results that can result in preventable, irreversible injury or death. [*See* Wilcox Decl. ¶13-17, 41-44, 51, 53-66, 68-70, 78-79, 81-94, 98-116, 119, 121-124, 133; Stewart Rep. ¶50-71, 73-84, 85-112] While much of this case rests on metrics and audits, behind those numbers are human beings who have suffered immeasurable harm and pain, and

Many of whom have died, as a result of Defendants' abject failures. Perhaps most illustrative of ADC's systemic failures and dangerous care is the case of, who mercifully was released from ASPC-Tucson in March 2016,

And is no longer dependent on Defendants for medical care. Mr. was diagnosed with testicular cancer in August 2015. [Wilcox Decl. 88] At every juncture, Defendants failed to provide Mr. with timely and appropriate care. His CT scan, ordered on an urgent basis, was performed weeks late on 9/23/15. [*Id.*] Mr. underwent surgery in late October 2015, and that is where his care essentially ended. [*Id.*] The follow-up CT

scan was not performed until November 24, 2015 and the consult notes attached to the CT were missing the pages that discussed the diagnosis and plan.29 [*Id.* ¶88-89] As such, Mr. received no care for biopsy-proven, CT-proven, surgical pathology-proven cancer. [*Id.* 89] Mr. is a young man with a highly treatable form of testicular cancer, but the appropriate treatment has to be done and it has to be done in a timely fashion.

Unfortunately, nothing about Mr. care has been timely, only recommended treatment has been accomplished, and there is no evidence that he was ever on anybody's radar within ADC because the last date he had a provider encounter was 10/30/2015—the date of his surgery. [*Id.* 90] He was never seen by a provider after returning to the facility prior to his release. [*Id.*]

Mr. Case is particularly troubling, for two reasons. First, Dr. Wilcox identified him to defendants in a face-to-face meeting in December 2015 as a patient in need of immediate attention for a potentially life-threatening illness, yet according to the medical record, he received virtually no attention in the ensuing three months. [*Id.* 91]

Second, Mr. Case is alarmingly similar to two other cases Dr. Wilcox reviewed at ASPC-Tucson, both involving young men with testicular cancer who experienced inexcusable delays in care. [*Id.* ¶13-15], died at age 42, on. After he underwent an orchiectomy (removal of his testicle), he should have immediately been placed under the care of an oncologist. In fact, he did not see an oncologist for five months, and when he did, he had widespread disease. [*Id.* 15] The ADC Mortality Review Committee concluded Mr. Death was preventable, and Dr. Wilcox agreed. [*Id.*] Similarly, thirty year old, experienced extreme delays in care for his testicular cancer, resulting in metastasis. Although he is still alive, he has been diagnosed as terminal, with less than a year to live. [*Id.* 14]

The suffering experienced prior to death by, a Yuma prisoner described above at pages 2-3, illustrates the suffering inflicted when patients cannot access basic nursing care.30 Despite Mr. serious conditions of end stage liver disease with fluid retention, groin wounds, and sepsis, the nursing staff repeatedly failed to respond to his desperate Health Needs Requests in March and April 2015, including at one point when he reported that his skin split open due to swelling, was infected, and swarmed with flies. [Wilcox Decl. ¶41-42] Shockingly, the nurse declined to see him. [*Id.* 42] More than a week after reporting the swarm of flies, he was finally transferred to the hospital, where he died. Dr. Wilcox agreed with the Mortality Review Committee's conclusion that multiple triage mistakes by nursing staff impeded and delayed Mr. Care, and concluded that the abysmal care hastened his death. [*Id.* 43] Patients in Defendants' infirmary units are particularly vulnerable and likely to suffer harm if not promptly seen. , died four days after arriving at ASPC-Tucson, without ever seeing a medical provider. [Wilcox Decl. 68] Mr. had a daily heroin habit and was placed in the infirmary to go through opiate withdrawal. Although seen by several nurses, who documented that he was experiencing serious withdrawal and was at risk of dehydration due to excessive vomiting, he was apparently never seen a medical provider,31 and was not prescribed IV medications for vomiting. [*Id.* ¶68, 78] Staff failed to monitor his condition, failed to order appropriate labs, and failed to refer him to a higher level of care. Consequently, Mr. died unnecessarily on, four days after his arrival at prison, at age 44. The Mortality Review Committee report correctly classified this as a preventable death. [*Id.* 68] A lack of timely access to provider's results in delayed or denied care, and places patients at substantial risk of harm. , died of leukemia at the age of 32 after Defendants failed to provide timely diagnostic care for almost a year. [*Id.* 103] She died four months after her diagnosis, and while Ms. may ultimately have succumbed to her illness, Dr. Wilcox determined without reservation that she experienced "repeated and inexcusable delays" in receiving a diagnosis and treatment for her leukemia, and that "these serious lapses resulted in hastening her death." [*Id.*] likewise suffered delays in care when she complained of radiating pain in her leg, abdominal pain, and the inability to urinate. Four days later, when her symptoms worsened and she could no longer use her legs, medical staff decided not to send her to a hospital but rather to the prison's medical clinic. While at the clinic,

Temperature registered at 91.9 degrees, a classic symptom of sepsis requiring emergency assessment. While she was eventually taken to the hospital, she died the next day from a staph infection, spinal meningitis, and pneumonia. Had her condition been properly triaged, she likely would have survived. Wilcox Decl. TT 53-54], experienced treatment delays at ASPC-Eyman in part because his very abnormal lab results apparently not reviewed by his provider for weeks. Mr. ultimately died, at the age of 43, with an infection of his heart. Had he been timely diagnosed, Dr. Wilcox opines he would not have died. Significant barriers remain in the provision of specially care for patients in Defendants' care. Essential coordination between Defendants' medical staff and outside specialists continues to fall well below the standard of care, with critical diagnostic results left ignored and unprocessed for extended periods of time."

EXPERTS FIND SYSTEM FLAWED

Various experts have found the system flawed but authorities refuse to take action.

Dr. Todd Wilcox [185] submitted his declaration and it reflects a seriously flawed system. Again the State Of Arizona Department Of Corrections with the approval of the Arizona legislature and the designated staff of the Arizona Attorney General's Office, have made it a practice to inflict torture on inmates.

He states at **2.** "This report assesses Arizona's prison medical care one year after the Court approved the parties' Stipulation settling this action. Under the Stipulation, defendants agreed to comply with 103 health care-related performance measures, to request that the Arizona Legislature approve a budget to allow ADC and its contracted health services vendor to modify the health services contract to increase health care staffing, and to implement additional policies and training programs."

3. "Through my three-day visit to Arizona State Prison Complex-Tucson on December 2-4, 2015, and my review of patient records, including death records, I have found that ADC prisoners continue to suffer serious harm, and in some cases preventable death, because defendants fail to provide necessary and timely health care on a systemwide basis. Tragically, this situation should come as a surprise to no one. The audits that Defendants have compiled every month since the Stipulation was entered document a system where patients lack reliable access to nurse triage, physicians, specialists, and/or necessary medication. The system is obviously broken, and human suffering is the unavoidable result"

7. "I reviewed all records for people who died in ADC custody during 2015 that were produced to me by 1/19/16. I reviewed patient healthcare records while visiting ASPC- Tucson and also reviewed records provided to me by plaintiffs' counsel. As was true for my previous reports, I did not review a random sample of records during my ASPC-Tucson site visit; instead, I chose to look at files of the same types of prisoners I reviewed for previous reports, including files for patients with diabetes, hypertension, HIV, kidney failure, hepatitis, infections and cancer. I also looked through lab reports, diagnostic test logs, and Health Needs Requests on site to identify patients who had objective findings that were concerning and then I asked for their charts to be pulled for my review. If I found areas of concern in the health care record, I frequently would request that the patient be pulled for me to interview to confirm my findings. I also interviewed patients I identified while on tours of the various housing units and then would review their charts afterward to gain additional information about their condition and the care plan. As I explained in previous reports, I focus my review on those patients with conditions requiring them to use the health care system."

9. "When I reviewed Arizona's prison medical care system in 2013 and 2014, I found that it was significantly below community standards and placed patients at serious risk of harm. Wilcox Reports, Doc. 1104-1 and 1138-1. Based upon my recent return visit at Tucson prison complex and my review of documents, my opinion has not changed. Prisoners in ADC custody continue to suffer an unreasonable risk of harm because the health care delivery system of their contractor, Corizon Health, Inc., is woefully deficient, and ADC officials do not acknowledge the gravity and impact of these deficiencies."

13. "Review of three similar cancer cases at one prison, ASPC-Tucson, vividly illustrates a system in disrepair. I discussed the case of in my Second Supplemental Report, served on defendants in September, 2014. Doc. 1138-1 at 165. He experienced unconscionable delays in screening and treatment for testicular cancer, a condition which, if treated timely is almost always curable. The 5-year survival rate of testicular cancer is approximately 95%. Siegel RL, Miller KD, Jemal A., Cancer statistics, 2015. CA Cancer J. Clin. 2015; 65:5. Declaration of Corene Kendrick, filed herewith, Ex. 4,3 PLTF-PARSONS-036248-36272. 14. Mr. 's complaints of testicular pain in mid-June, 2013 were essentially ignored, and despite a urology recommendation for a radical orchiectomy(removal of the testicle) in September, 2013, the surgery was not provided until 3/24/14. Ex. 60 at ADC418740, ADC418712, 418718, 418740. I noted previously that this delay has exposed Mr. to an unreasonable risk of harm. Doc. 1138-1 at 165. I interviewed Mr. recently while at Tucson complex on 12/4/15, and reviewed his current medical record. Tragically, but predictably, the cancer has spread to his lungs and has been deemed inoperable and untreatable. Sadly, Mr. who is 30 years old, has now been diagnosed as terminal, and has less than a year to live. He will die of a treatable and curable disease. In a healthy medical care system, I would expect that the identification of a case with the inexcusable and dangerous health care delays identified in Mr. 's case would trigger a review of the case history and remedial measures to ensure that the deficiencies in Mr. 's case do not recur for future patients.

15. Sadly, Mr. 's case was not an isolated aberration. In addition to his case, I found two other cases of testicular cancer in young men who suffered unconscionable delays in care. , died of testicular cancer

on less than a month shy of his 43rd birthday. Mr. sought care for an enlarged testicle in June, 2014. He underwent an orchiectomy (removal of his testicle) in September, 2014, just days after my report was submitted. He should have seen an oncologist immediately after this procedure, but he did not. Indeed, I found no documentation from the hospital following the orchiectomy, and it appears he received virtually no medical attention for the three months following the surgery. He was not seen by an oncologist until five months after the surgery, on 2/12/15. On 10/20/15 he underwent surgery to remove lymph nodes and the surgeons found that he had widespread cancer in major blood vessels. He ultimately died of shock resulting from a severe postoperative bleed. The ADC's Mortality Review Committee concluded, correctly, that Mr. 's death was preventable. Ex. 69 at ADCM228197-199.

16. Twenty-seven year old may be the next victim. Counsel for plaintiffs found Mr. by speaking to random prisoners at cell front while walking through a housing unit, and brought his complaints to my attention. I interviewed him and reviewed his health records, which confirmed his allegations of inadequate care. He started complaining of testicular pain in July 2015. He was initially scheduled to have an orchiectomy on 9/30/15. However, because nobody within the Arizona Department of Corrections or Corizon communicated appropriately, he was fed breakfast that morning and thus his surgery had to be cancelled. It took the system an additional month to get him scheduled for his necessary care, and he had an orchiectomy on 10/30/15.

17. Because of the urgency of his condition, the surgeon ordered a postoperative appointment two weeks later to review pathology, postoperative imaging and to refer him to an oncologist. As of 12/4/15 when I interviewed him, he had not seen an oncologist to consider chemotherapy and radiation. During my prison visit, I notified ADC officials and their attorneys of Mr. 's critical needs. Since visiting Tucson, I reviewed more recent documents from his medical file dated through 2/10/16. Despite the alarm that I raised to ADC staff during the tour of Mr. 's critical need for immediate health care, he still has not received chemotherapy or seen an oncologist, as discussed in more detail in Part II.D.3 below. If provided proper care, Mr. 's condition is curable and he would be able to survive this occurrence of cancer. Given the unconscionable delays and incompetence that appear to be standard in these three cases, I fear he will not.

A. Death Reviews

18. I reviewed medical records and corresponding mortality reviews, when available, for 72 ADC prisoners who died and for whom defendants produced medical records through January, 2016. In most cases, the records I received covered roughly the year leading up to the patient's death. From the 72, I identified 57 files that contained sufficient records to evaluate the quality of care, for patients who died of natural causes. Of these cases, I conclude that 21 prisoners (37%) received grossly deficient care. Tragically, in 11 cases, it is likely that the patient would have lived had he or she received timely adequate care. Ten other cases had significant deficits in care, including delays in diagnosis and delays in obtaining definitive care. Even where the deaths were not preventable, the deficient care resulted in patients enduring unnecessary pain and suffering and resulted in a significant shortening of lifespan.

19. As detailed below, a substantial proportion of the problematic deaths involved health care delivery system failures, including limited access to care based on an insufficient number of qualified providers and nurses; unreliable chronic care programs; failure to provide timely access to specialty care and, when patients do see a specialist, failure to timely follow-up to implement the specialist's recommendations; and failure to effectively track and monitor lab and diagnostic test results. While one or two of these types of deaths in a large system could be considered aberrant, the number and quality of the problematic cases in ADC in 2015 reveal a system that is fundamentally dysfunctional and dangerous. As discussed below, this finding is entirely consistent with the state's own CGAR monitoring scores.

C. Timely access to care

37. As I explained in earlier reports, access to care, *i.e.,* the task of getting patients to see nurses and providers is a basic building block in the structure of a functional health care system. Arizona failed at this fundamental task two years ago when I first evaluated the system, and it fails today. Having interviewed ASPC-Tucson patients and reviewed an extensive number of medical records from Tucson and other facilities, I found a shocking number of delays in access to care and complete denials of care in Arizona's prisons. These delays and denials harm some patients and place all patients at an unreasonable risk of serious harm."

53. At Perryville, for example, I found two tragic cases where staff simply failed to recognize that their patients were suffering life-threatening conditions requiring emergency care. who had a history of deep vein thrombosis (blood clots), pulmonary embolus (blockages in her lungs), abscesses and osteomyelitis (bone infection). On 9/6/15, she complained of radiating pain down her leg, abdominal pain and the inability to urinate. Although she was able to void after receiving IV fluids that day, she was unable to urinate the following day. The standard of care in this situation requires an immediate and full assessment to determine whether the patient is in renal failure or has a different condition interfering with urination. Instead, on 9/8/15,

Ms. was given Flomax, a drug that was inappropriate, and Toradol, a drug that was actually contraindicated and potentially dangerous.

54. The next day, she complained of chest pain and the inability to move her legs. Instead of sending her offsite for emergency care, which was clearly warranted, Ms. was taken to the prison's central medical clinic, where her temperature was recorded as 91.9 degrees Fahrenheit, which is a critical vital sign abnormality suggestive of sepsis and requiring emergency assessment. She was eventually taken to the hospital, where she died the following day of a staph infection, spinal meningitis and pneumonia. Ex. 68 at ADCM228194. Had she been sent to the hospital emergently on 9/6/15, her infections would have been treated sooner and she very likely would have survived. The Mortality Review Committee's report indicates that her presentation was confusing and concludes that her care met community care standards. Ex. 68 at ADCM228195-96. For the reasons explained above, I strongly disagree.

55. Another woman, clearly should have been sent offsite for emergency care when she fell from her bed early in the morning on and staff found her with bloody fecal matter on her legs and body, a racing pulse and alarmingly low blood pressure. The on-call nurse practitioner ordered Ms. Be taken to Perryville's central medical complex, where she was provided an IV, but her blood pressure continued to drop. Her blood pressure fell dramatically at the complex, and she clearly required emergency care. Instead, despite her life-threatening blood pressure readings, Ms. was returned to her housing unit by nursing staff after receiving her IV fluids. Ex. 26 at ADCM228173. Shockingly, the practitioner did not document an abdominal exam or any explanation for the fecal matter on her body. In the late afternoon that same day, custody staff called another ICS (ADC code for emergency incident) when they noticed Ms. had vomited blood. *Id.* Although her blood pressure again was dangerously low, the staff did not call for an emergency transport for almost 40 minutes. She died shortly thereafter. The ADC Mortality Review Committee classified this death as preventable, and I agree. Ex. 26 at ADCM228171. The emergency response and decision making were beneath the standard of care and the delay in definitive care proved fatal.

56. , a patient at ASPC-Lewis with a history of Type 2 diabetes, should have been sent to a hospital on when he reported left sided chest pain with radiation into his neck, left arm and left shoulder blade. He also was sweating heavily and short of breath. He also had very low blood pressure and a racing pulse. Ex. 57 at ADCM196768. Seen together, these are signs of serious cardiac pain. Rather than send him to a hospital emergency room for lab tests, the nurse treating him had labs drawn at the prison and waited hours for the results, a treatment decision clearly beyond the nurse's scope of practice. When they were reported as abnormal, Mr. was taken to the hospital in the mid-afternoon, where he died the following day. Although his record is limited, it is very likely that the delay in providing him with definitive care and nursing staff's decision to delay his emergency transport hastened his death.

57. The MRC report recognized the delay, and recommended an in-service training on assessment, evaluation and treatment of chest pain. Ex. 57 at ADCM196770. While I agree that training in this case is certainly warranted, the care in this case is so grossly substandard that it warrants an investigation to determine whether employee discipline is appropriate.

58. illustrates the tragic consequences of poor access to the appropriate level of health care and the disorganization of the electronic medical record system. Mr. died on of a gallbladder infection that would have been easily treated had he received timely care. Instead, the last three months of his life were marred by a series of lapses and missteps, including three mishandled emergencies, that resulted in the denial of medically necessary care.

59. Mr. who suffered from very poorly controlled diabetes (Ex. 31 at ADCM172397), developed alarming symptoms that should have prompted a thorough work up. He submitted an HNR on 4/6/15 complaining of blood in his urine. *Id.* At ADCM173275. Lab tests dated 4/9/15 revealed multiple critically abnormal values demonstrating significant liver dysfunction, but the record contains no indication that these results were ever communicated to Mr. 's physician at the time they were received. The patient's labs were reviewed on 4/16/15 and the critically abnormal tests were acknowledged. *Id.* at ADCM172737. The patient was seen by a gastroenterologist on 4/30/15 but the consultant's report was not reviewed by his physician until three weeks later (ADCM172430), resulting in delayed implementation of critical care recommendations.

60. Mr. was becoming increasingly ill, resulting in custody calling three ICS's in a period of ten days. The first ICS, on 5/27/15, was based on his shortness of breath. The healthcare provider who examined him noted he was short of breath, his abdomen was distended with ascites and he had 3+ edema in his legs (*Id.* At ADCM172790). The provider failed to recognize the severity of this patient's new symptoms and merely ordered him a diuretic and a 1-month followup. *Id.* At ADCM172793.

61. The second ICS was called on 6/4/15, at which point an RN documented that he had full body pain, swelling and hyperactive bowel sounds. Although the nurse writes that the physician examined the patient, there are no exam notes by a physician in the record. The patient was prescribed Tylenol, which was contraindicated in light of his liver failure, and was likely ineffective for his pain. *Id.* at ADCM173216.

62. The following day, Mr. was assessed by an LPN, who performed a complete examination of the patient, despite the fact that this level of care is well out of her scope of licensure. Although she referred the patient's chart for provider review, there is no evidence that the review occurred. *Id.* at ADCM173212.

63. Finally, on 6/6/15, a third ICS was called. The RN noted that Mr. had a critical lab value. At this point, the Nurse Practitioner ordered him transferred to the outside hospital. It is unclear what critical lab value prompted this transfer because there are no orders for labs in this date range (*id.* at ADCM172725), there are no lab reports from this date range in the medical record, the LPN note does not indicate what lab value was critical (*id.* at ADCM173204), and the practitioner who received the critical lab value (NP Mulhern) did not put a note in the chart indicating what critical information was conveyed to her.

64. Overall Mr. s care was disorganized, delayed, haphazard, and inadequate and the sum total of his treatment does not meet the standard of care. His medical record is extremely confusing and I agree with the Mortality Review Committee that his course of care was difficult to follow because of what was documented, what occurred and was not documented, and what was documented in the wrong sections. The provider failed to work up the sudden and significant changes in his health status and the provider's oversight of the healthcare team was delayed and inappropriate. This patient had critical labs that were never addressed, major changes in his bloodwork, multiple ICS responses with ominous physical exam findings that were completely ignored, and consults that gave appropriate guidance that were not reviewed or implemented in a timely fashion to facilitate his workup. While it is clear that he had a number of tests and consults completed during this three month span, the care was so fragmented and scattered that nobody really put together the overall picture of his healthcare issues. By the time he was finally transferred to the hospital, he was so physically sick and compromised that his treatment at the hospital was ineffective and limited and he ultimately had fatal medical complications as a result. The ADC Mortality Review Committee concluded that it could not determine whether this death was preventable. Ex. 30 at ADCM173601. Had Mr. been properly worked up in April 2015, I believe he might have survived.

65. I encountered in the inpatient unit at ASPCTucson. He is an insulin-dependent diabetic who has had a kidney transplant. He has also had a right leg amputation, finger amputation and he was in the IPC with a diagnosis of Fournier's Gangrene. This diagnosis was given to him by the Corizon physician. There is a note on 12/1/2015 from Dr. Burciaga indicating that he had Fournier's Gangrene and he was to be a direct admit to Mt. Vista Hospital with Dr. D'Silva accepting on 12/1/2015. However, when we toured on 12/2/2015 he was still in his prison bed. This is a problem because Fournier's Gangrene is a surgical emergency that carries a very high morbidity rate. Usually surgery is required to save the patient's life within hours after diagnosis and hyperbaric oxygen treatment is frequently necessary as well. So it is appropriate that Dr. Burciaga sent him to be a direct admit to the hospital; it is completely inappropriate for this emergency case to have waited. In my brief time at Tucson, I was not able to identify the reason for this inexcusable delay. I suspect that it is related to staffing – had Tucson allocated sufficient health care staff to the inpatient unit in which Mr. is housed, someone would have been tasked with ensuring his prompt transfer. The failure to timely transfer him greatly increased his chances of requiring yet another amputation or of dying. This is abysmal care."

2. Use of nurses as primary care providers

77. Patients are denied a clinician's professional medical judgment if nurses or other staff are called upon to make decisions they are not qualified to make or exceed professional licensing requirements. I reported that this was a significant problem in my first report, and it continues to occur, placing patients at serious risk of harm or death.

78. As discussed in paragraph 68 above, was in crisis during his brief stay in the infirmary, leading up to his death. He should have been under the care of a provider who was seeing him regularly while he withdrew from his daily heroin habit. Instead, he was repeatedly seen by LPNs and RNs who assessed his condition, but failed to address it or to refer him to a provider who was qualified to treat his life-threatening condition.

79. Patient died on at age 55 at ASPC-Tucson, after his cancer of the head and neck recurred. When he reported his symptoms returning, he was seen for sick call by an LPN on 12/29/2014, rather than an RN, who noted his history of optic nerve cancer, but failed to refer him to a provider. Ex. 71 at ADCM118615-20. Mr. was finally seen by a provider and, on 5/11/15 by an oncologist who diagnosed him with recurrence of his cancer via PET scan. He was ordered to have chemotherapy ASAP. ADCM120514. Although he was finally provided treatment after seeing the oncologist, his recurrent cancer was in an advanced state, and he declined rapidly. While he may have died in any case, the delay in seeing a provider, and subsequently an oncologist, certainly shortened his life. The mortality report indicates that this care met community standards and I disagree. Ex. 83 at ADCM196779-82. The delays in care certainly do not meet community standards, nor does assessment of possible recurrent cancer by a Licensed Practical Nurse.

3. Specialty care

80. The exercise of professional judgment sometimes requires more in-depth knowledge than primary care providers possess. In these cases, the provider must be able to refer patients for specialty consultations. This essential step often was not happening two years ago, when I first reviewed care, and there continue to be major barriers for specialty access. In addition, the specialists who see the prisoners are authorized to recommend treatment, but not to order it. Thus, it is critical that the prison health care system ensures that prison health care providers promptly review the consultant's treatment recommendations and either order the treatment or document why it is not appropriate. This essential coordination is often missing in ADC patient care.

81. The failure to ensure that patients see specialty consultants for medically necessary diagnosis and treatment places patients at an unreasonable risk of harm. Indeed, in some cases, patients will die because they did not have access to medically necessary specialty care. Sixty-five year old for example, was referred multiple times to a cardiologist while at ASPC-Eyman, but the appointments did not occur timely because of multiple operational glitches in the referral process and lack of communication between the referring clinicians and the approval authority. Ex. 45 at ADCM135400. He was ultimately referred for an implantable defibrillator, but he died on before that visit was arranged. Had his diagnostic consults been approved by Utilization Management and scheduled in a timely manner, he would likely still be alive. The ADC Mortality Review reached the same conclusion. *Id.*

82. I spoke to a number of Tucson prisoners regarding longstanding barriers to specialty care, and brought their urgent situations to the attention of ADC officials, and their attorneys. Thirty-two year old , was a patient in the Tucson infirmary when I spoke to him. He had been placed there after he developed a decubitus ulcer on his buttocks as a result of long-standing diarrhea caused by an infection in his GI tract. Although the infection had been identified more than a year earlier, I found no evidence that he had ever been treated for it. Moreover, he had been referred to general surgery to repair the wound on 6/25/15, but has been told that Corizon has not been able to find a surgeon with whom to schedule surgery. In the meantime this otherwise relatively healthy young man has been bedridden for months.

83. 78 years old, has a transplanted kidney and has been on his immunosuppression medications for many years. He developed an allergy to one of his medications that is causing him to have a terrible whole-body rash. His medical record shows he has submitted many HNR's about his issues and Corizon has not sent him to a transplant physician for evaluation. As a result, he stopped taking his Prograf and Cellsept on 10/29/2015 because the rash had become so intolerable. Instead of sending him to a transplant physician as medically indicated, Corizon referred him for a psychiatric consult to see if he is competent. In conversing with this gentleman it was obvious that he is intellectually keen and well informed about his situation. Competency is not the issue in this case and a referral to psychiatry to assess competency for refusing to take medication is a shameless cover-your-behind maneuver by the prescriber that clearly demonstrates that the provider did not speak to Mr. in any detail, and does not know how to deal with a patient of his complexity. Mr. 's providers have failed to understand that he urgently needs to go see a transplant physician to manage his medications and to assess the kidney. Without this care, he will undoubtedly reject his kidney, which will ultimately hasten his death.

84. Patient is a 47 year old ASPC-Tucson patient with sick sinus syndrome and Wolf-Parkinson-White Syndrome, a condition that causes rapid heartbeat. He has had a pacemaker placed and has had two cardiac ablations. He has had such bad complications from his disease that he filed for a restraining order against Corizon and forced them to house him in IPC because his heart rate fluctuates, and he loses consciousness. He indicates that his cardiology consult to address this was submitted by his provider in August 2015 and he has yet to be seen. Review of his chart demonstrates that despite his multiple issues, his chronic care appointments were just not done and he has not been seen in a timely fashion.

85. Patient, is a 25 year old who developed a slipped disc in his back. While at ASPC-Lewis, he submitted HNRs about this but his care was delayed. Ultimately, he became paralyzed and incontinent before he was finally sent to the hospital for treatment. This constitutes abysmal care. He has a lot of residual nerve damage and can only walk short distances because of weakness and balance issues. When I reviewed his medical record, it stated that he was transferred to Tucson from Lewis in order to receive physical therapy. None had occurred as of my December visit, and he is understandably upset that he has not made progress towards independence.

86. Another Tucson prisoner, underwent an above knee amputation April 2015. No prosthesis had been provided to him, so when I met him he was stuck in a wheelchair despite the fact that he is otherwise physically vigorous and could be up walking which would be much healthier for him and enable him to keep his muscle mass in his legs. He was sent back to the prison following his amputation and was not seen by his provider for five months. Then, on 10/19/15 a consult for a prosthesis was submitted, but that appointment has not yet occurred. When we interviewed the "consult specialist" for Corizon, she verified the consult was approved, but had no explanation for the delay in scheduling the appointment.

87. Finally, Mr. the young man with testicular cancer who I described at the beginning of this report, has experienced unconscionable delays in receiving treatment even after I first brought him to the attention of ADC during the tour in early December 2015. Plaintiffs' counsel randomly met him while walking through a housing unit at Tucson, speaking cellfront with prisoners, and while I was at Tucson I reviewed his medical records and spoke with him. I also raised his case in a meeting with ADC staff and their attorneys on the last day of the tour. Since visiting Tucson, I received updated medical records for him, up until 2/10/16. These records clearly demonstrate the colossal systemic issues that exist within the ADC healthcare system.

88. Mr. was originally diagnosed with testicular cancer by ultrasound on 8/6/15. Ex. 67 at ADCM340110. An urgent request for a CT scan was submitted to Corizon Utilization Management by Dr. Goodman at the time, but that was not completed until 9/23/15. Ex. 67 at ADCM340368. Mr. was subsequently scheduled for an orchiectomy on 10/30/15. In the discharge plans for that surgery, the surgeon (Dr. Daley) requested a two week follow-up after the surgery, along with a CT scan so the pathology could be reviewed and the tumor could be staged appropriately to determine additional care. The specialist's request for a follow-up consult and CT scan was submitted by Dr. Goodman, and she indicated the ordered timelines. Unfortunately, Corizon did not complete the CT scan until 11/24/15, and the post-op follow-up with Dr. Daley was not until 12/2/15, more than a month after the surgery. *Id.* at ADCM340344.

89. Critically, only one out of three pages of the specialty consult report from Dr. Daley inexplicably is included in the medical file. *Id.* at ADCM340349. The pages that are notably missing are those that detail the diagnosis and the plan. Furthermore, I can find no evidence in the medical record that a provider at the prison reviewed the incomplete specialist report from Dr. Daley, to realize that the most critical components of the note were missing. As such, Mr. has had no care for biopsy-proven, CT-proven, surgical pathology-proven cancer.

90. Since the appropriate documentation does not exist in the chart and we have no idea what the plan was for Mr. 's care, we have to rely on the data that does exist. I know that he had a pure seminoma and that he has CT-proven evidence of mediastinal (chest) adenopathy that measures 2.1 cm x 2.0 cm. *Id.* at ADCM339817. Applying a standard grading scale to this scenario, this patient has a Grade IIB tumor. *See* Oh, W.K., Overview of the treatment of testicular germ cell tumors; Uptodate, Kantoff, PW (ed), Waltham MA (accessed March 28, 2016), available at http://www.uptodate.com/contents/overview-of-the-treatment-of-testicular-germ-celltumors. The current treatment recommendations for a Grade IIB seminoma are surgery to remove tumor (already done) and chemotherapy (not done). *Id.* Seminomas are a highly treatable and generally curable form of testicular cancer, but the appropriate treatment has to be done and it has to be done in a timely fashion. Unfortunately, nothing about Mr. 's care has been timely, only part of the recommendation treatment has been accomplished, and there is no evidence that he is on anybody's radar within ADOC because the last date he had a provider encounter was 10/30/2015—the date of his surgery. Ex. 67 at ADCM339815. He has never been seen by a provider since returning to the facility.

91. We encountered Mr. on my tour of the Tucson facility. I was so concerned at the time after I reviewed his file on-site about his lack of care that I made a request to conduct an exit conference meeting on 12/4/15 to call his situation (and the critical situations of several other patients) to the attention of Corizon administrators and health care staff. I was clear with the ADC attorneys about the purpose of the meeting and the seriousness of the issues. Unfortunately, despite my clarity about the purpose of the exit conference, not a single staff person from Corizon showed up to hear my concerns about Mr. and other prisoners, and my concerns were directed to ADC monitoring staff and attorneys for Defendants. As such, my admonitions for Mr. to have emergency oncology consultation and treatment went unheeded, and he never received appropriate care. I am professionally disturbed by this case because he is a young man who has a very treatable and curable condition that is being totally mismanaged, and Corizon and the ADOC know of his situation. If anybody with clinical training had looked at his chart and tracked his care, the deficits in care would have been obvious. Unfortunately, Corizon's healthcare delivery is so broken that this patient's life is on the line from systemic incompetence despite my detailed description of his problems and his needed care.

92. Mr. also attempted to call his situation to the attention of Corizon officials. He submitted an HNR on 12/29/15 stating "I was supposed to see the oncologist over a month ago for treatment. I need to know what's going on." *Id.* at ADCM340317. This HNR was responded to on 12/29/15 by RN Rynders with "You are scheduled for f/u with the provider." This HNR never made it into the master list of Health Services Requests, (*Id.* at ADCM339817), and as of February 10, 2016 he still had not seen a provider.

93. Mr. submitted another HNR on 1/16/16 that stated "I need to speak to Doctor Goodman ASAP. I was supposed to be scheduled to seen an oncologist over two months ago to start my chemotherapy treatment but I haven't heard a thing back so I need to know what is going on very soon!!!" *Id.* at ADCM340315. This HNR was responded to on 1/18/16 by RN Rynders stating that "You are scheduled to see the Provider." This HNR is not recorded in the master list of "Health Services Requests" and it appears that it never got implemented, because there is no evidence he ever saw a provider despite the serious nature of the HNR request. *Id.* at ADCM339817.

1. Providers' orders

118. Orders written by providers must actually be carried out. Throughout the Arizona system I saw a consistent pattern of ordered care – medications, labs, nursing care, follow-up appointments, and/or specialty referrals – not getting done. This is another symptom of a badly understaffed medical care system.

119. While at ASPC-Tucson, I spoke to a number of patients who were referred for specialty care who never received it, and had predictably poor outcomes. For example, , was bedridden in the infirmary unit with a decubitus ulcer resulting from long-standing diarrhea caused by a C. Difficile infection in his GI tract. His ulcer was not healing because of an exposed vein in the base of the wound that kept bleeding. I asked Mr. why he had not had the relatively common surgery for decubitus ulcers to deal with this problem definitively. He indicated that the Corizon staff had told him they could not find a surgeon willing to treat him. I confirmed in his medical chart that a 6/25/15 surgery referral request for wound care had not been carried out. The surgery that he needs is routine and not that difficult. Any competent plastic surgeon would handle his issue easily. It is difficult to believe that no surgeon is willing to treat him unless the problem is with payment from Corizon for that care.

120. During the Tucson visit, I also observed that the process for alerting providers to diagnostic test results and consult reports for their patients through the electronic medical record had essentially collapsed under its own weight. Because providers daily receive dozens of emails, and because the process for signing off on results was unduly time-consuming and inefficient, many of the providers had simply allowed their mail boxes to fill without reviewing them. I observed that Tucson's NP Daye, for example, had almost 2,500 unread emails in her inbox on the day of my visit, many of which were lab results and specialist's reports. Dr. Burciaga had approximately 5,600 unread clinical emails in her inbox. Reviewing medical records at the facility, I found numerous examples of cases where patients with abnormal labs were never followed up, and where patients who saw the consultant did not receive the recommended treatment because the consult reports had not been reviewed by the provider.

121. Mr. , discussed above, required monitoring for the immunosuppressive medication, tacrolimus, which he takes to maintain his transplanted kidney. His provider ordered a STAT tacrolimus lab drawn 11/27/15—there was no result in the chart by 12/2/15 which is an unacceptable delay for a STAT lab. That result should be back within hours. On 9/3/15 a regular tacrolimus level was ordered and a result was delivered 9/8/15. This lab result was never reviewed by anyone. The failure to review these lab results, and the failure to obtain timely results for a STAT order, put the patient at significant risk of harm.

122. The failure to follow orders can produce tragic results, as demonstrated in the case of who died on at age 50 at ASPC-Florence. Mr. had a history of renal failure, type II diabetes, cirrhosis, foot amputation, and peripheral vascular disease. It appears that he was significantly compromised when transferred to the Department of Corrections on 6/10/15. He was evaluated by a physician on 6/12/15 and sent immediately to the hospital as a direct admit for a high white blood cell count and a draining left foot amputation wound. Mr. was stabilized at the hospital but noted to be in acute renal failure. That was addressed at the hospital, and he was discharged back to ADC on

6/17/15, and his discharge plan included prescriptions for critical medications. Although these medications were ordered by prison staff on 6/17/15, he did not receive a dose until 6/20/15. Ex. 37 at ADCM107446, 107448. Without these medications, Mr. decompensated quickly and was ultimately admitted into the infirmary. On the infirmary nurses called Dr. Vukcevic at 11:35 to inform him that Mr. was not doing well. Instead of sending this critically ill patient back to the hospital immediately, Dr. Vukcevic instructed nursing staff to apply supplemental oxygen and to continue to observe him. The doctor stated he would be in within an hour to assess the patient. However at 12:55 Mr. was declared dead and the treating physician at the time was Dr. Chris Johnson. *Id.* at ADCM107543. Dr. Vukcevic never came to assess the patient who he blocked from going to the emergency room.

123. This case raises a number of questions. First of all it appears that Mr. was significantly medically compromised at the time and he was transferred to the Department of Corrections and I have no way of knowing where he came from or how it was possible for someone to transfer a patient this sick to ADC. This case also raises questions about the intake process at the ADC reception center and its capacity to identify patients who are too sick to be in a prison environment. Furthermore, this case shows a failure to coordinate care when a very sick patient transfers from the hospital back to the prison. Here, he was ordered critical medication at the hospital as part of his discharge plan but went three days without that medication upon transfer back to the prison, ultimately causing him to destabilize and contributing to his death. I also question the delay in emergency care, and why the physician did not send this patient to the hospital immediately upon hearing that he was having difficulty. Clearly Dr. Vukcevic's instructions were inadequate for this patient, and the delay in obtaining definitive care proved fatal. Given the magnitude of Mr. 's medical conditions his death was inevitable. However it is clear that systemic issues abound in this case and his care was compromised significantly as a result. I concur with the ADC Mortality Review finding that "more timely intervention was clearly warranted." Ex. 38 at ADCM130868.

124. In the charts I reviewed at Tucson, and the charts of deceased prisoners from across the prisons, I saw that labs are routinely ordered but never done, medications ordered but not approved, medications ordered but not administered by the nurses, ADA accommodations ordered but not provided, consults ordered but never approved or scheduled, and follow-up appointments requested by providers but never scheduled. Recommendations from specialists regarding follow-up and additional care were frequently not done or were substantially delayed. Tucson prisoner , , for example, has a condition, inclusion body myositis, which results in significant weakness of his muscles. Tucson referred him to a neurologist, who recommended on 4/16/14 that he be provided a back brace, supportive shoes, elevated shower chair, handicapped bed rails with bars, a multi-vitamin per day, a wedge pillow, an electric hospital bed, and a wheelchair assessment. NP Daye finally ordered these items for him on 11/10/15, a year and a half later. Corizon's Utilization Management Department has denied all of the requests for these medical devices.

2. Medication administration and monitoring

125. Prescribed medications must be provided to patients in a timely, consistent manner. The ADC monitor reports document consistent and persistent problems delivering medications to patients on time. Performance Measure # 11 requires that new prescriptions be provided to the patient within two business days of the prescription, or the same day, if prescribed STAT. The average scores over the

months of February through December, 2015 were below 75% at six of the ten prisons, including at all five of the largest men's prisons. The chart on the next page highlights in yellow each month in 2015 where the prison's compliance level was less than 75%. For each month in 2015, the statewide level of compliance for all of ten institutions.

126. Medications must be renewed regularly and without interruption, and prisoners must be able to transfer housing locations without medication interruptions. ADC monitors' reports show that administration of prescription medication is frequently delayed or missed, and that prescriptions for chronic care medications frequently lapse despite the patients refill requests.

127. As a preliminary matter, I have long maintained that, in a prison or jail setting, an automatic refill system for chronic care and psychotropic medications is critical, and I so advised the parties in this action. ADC's system of requiring patients, some of whom are on psychotropic medications for disabling mental conditions, to file health needs requests to refill their prescriptions practically guarantees they will have gaps in receiving medications. This is particularly true in a system like ADC's, as the Corizon pharmacy responsible for filling the prescriptions is not local, but in Oklahoma.

128. Performance Measure # 14 requires that refills of chronic care and psychotropic medications requested by the patient three to seven days before the medication runs out are filled so that the patient will suffer no lapse. Not one of the ten prisons averaged a passing score (75%) for this measure over the ten months from March to December 2015. (Every facility was given a score of "NA" in February 2015.) Again, non-compliance is shown in yellow in the chart below. Ex. 1 at PLTF-PARSONS-036223.

129. ASPC-Lewis registered a 0% compliance rate for nine of the ten months, and only three small prisons, Phoenix, Safford and Winslow, had an average score of over 50%. Of the five largest prisons, not a single one achieved a passing score at any time during the measured period. As illustrated below, none of the ten prisons achieved a passing average score during the relevant time period. Ex. 1 at PLTF-PARSONS-036223.

130. ADC's record for ensuring that prescriptions for chronic care and psychotropic medications are renewed by the prescribing provider, such that there are no lapses, is also dismal. (Performance Measure # 13.) For the eleven month period of February to December 2015, seven of the prisons, including all of the largest facilities, had average scores well under 75% compliance, as illustrated in the chart on the next page. Ex. 1 at PLTF-PARSONS-036222.

3. Labs, imaging, and other diagnostic tests

131. Diagnostic tests are an essential part of any medical care system. Such tests must be performed timely, based on the provider's order, and must be reviewed and, if abnormal, acted upon promptly. Arizona fails all too often to ensure that labs and diagnostic tests performed are promptly reviewed and acted upon, due in part to the lack of an effective system for reporting such results in the eOMIS system.

132. Once the diagnostic reports are available, the medical provider is required to review the reports, including pathology reports, and act upon those with abnormal values within five calendar days. (Performance Measure # 46.) Nine out of ten of the prisons averaged scores well below passing for this measure, from February to December, 2015. Indeed, the only prison that averaged a passing score was ASPC-Safford, a smaller prison that ADC previously has reported does not house prisoners with high medical needs. *See, e.g.,*

Ex. 11 at ADCM226253 (11/30/15) (at Florence's, North unit, just one report of 10 reviewed timely, with half not reviewed a month or more after receipt; Central unit, only half of 10 reports timely reviewed, with three not reviewed six weeks after receipt); Ex. 16 at ADCM226321 (11/27/15) (at Tucson, in Inpatient Unit, only half of ten records in audit showed timely review); Ex. 13 at ADCM226171 (11/25/15) (at Perryville, San Pedro unit, for ten pap smear tests, only one had result timely reviewed).

133. The failure to act timely on abnormal labs and diagnostic imaging places patients and enormous risk of harm. Given ADC's widespread non-compliance on this measure, it is not surprising that I found numerous examples of patients who were suffering unnecessarily because their providers had failed to act upon their abnormal results. Among them was Mr. (see *infra* at ¶82 and 119), who tested positive for C. Difficile toxin on 9/18/14. There was no evidence in his record that the results were ever reviewed, or that Mr. was ever treated for this condition. *See also*, Ex. 54 at ADCM086498 (high white blood cell count for Mr. 096480, suggestive of infection performed 5/27/15, not signed off by provider until 6/16/15; patient died eleven days later); (per my onsite chart review, STAT test for immunosuppressant ordered 11/27/15 for Mr. 073659, not performed as of 12/2/15; regular lab ordered 9/3/15, performed 9/8/15, results never reviewed).

III. Conclusion

Medical care in Arizona prisons continues to be inadequate to meet the basic needs of many of the prisoners who experience illness and injury while in custody. Many of the barriers to care that I identified in November 2013, and in my subsequent reports, continue to plague the system. ADC's own audits demonstrate month after month that many of the prisons are failing to comply with critical performance measures, even at the first year level of 75%. Fewer still will meet the current 80% benchmark. The treatment delays and backlogs point to a shortage of health care staff that must be remedied to create an adequate health care system. Defendants should be required (1) to immediately develop a plan to increase nurse and physician staffing to enable each prison to achieve passing CGAR scores of at least 80% for access to RN triage, primary care and chronic care appointments (Performance Measures # 37, # 39 and # 54), timely inpatient encounters (Performance Measure # 66) and timely provider review of diagnostic test results (Performance Measure # 46) ; and (2) to develop a plan to perform a workload study for all health care positions, and to create and implement a staffing plan based upon the results of the study. Additionally, they should be required to develop a plan to automatically refill prescriptions for chronic care and psychiatric diagnoses.

Prenatal Services 57 A Medical Provider will order prenatal vitamins and diet for a pregnant inmate at the inmate's initial intake physical examination.

Prenatal Services 58 Results of an inmate's prenatal screening tests will be documented in the medical record.

Preventative Services 59 Inmates will be screened for TB on an annual basis.

Preventative Services 60 All female inmates ages 21 to 65 will be offered a Pap smear at the inmate's initial intake physical examination.

Preventative Services 61 All female inmates ages 21 to 65 will be offered a Pap smear , every 36 months after initial intake, unless more frequent screening is clinically recommended.

Preventative Services 62 All prisoners are screened for tuberculosis upon intake.

Infirmary Care 63 In an IPC, an initial health assessment will be completed by a Registered Nurse on the date of admission.

Infirmary Care 64 In an IPC, a Medical Provider evaluation and plan will occur within the next business day after admission.

Infirmary Care 65 In an IPC, a written history and physical examination will be completed by a medical provider within 72 hours of admission.

Infirmary Care 66 In an IPC, a Medical Provider encounters will occur at a minimum every 72 hours.

Infirmary Care 67 In an IPC, Registered nurses will conduct and document an assessment at least once every shift. Graveyard shift assessments can be welfare checks.

Infirmary Care 68 In an IPC, Inmate health records will include admission orders and documentation of care and treatment given.

Infirmary Care 69 In an IPC, nursing care plans will be reviewed weekly documented with a date and signature.

Infirmary Care 70 All IPC patients have properly working call buttons, and if not, health care staff perform and document 30-minute patient welfare checks.

Medical Diets 71 Inmates with diagnosed and documented diseases or conditions that necessitate a special diet will be provided the diet, if clinically indicated. When prescribing the special diet, the provider will include the type of diet, duration for which it is to be provided, and any special instructions.

Medical Diets 72 Inmates who refuse prescribed diets for more than 3 consecutive days will receive follow-up nutritional counseling by a QHCP.

Mental Health 73 All MH-3 minor prisoners shall be seen by a licensed mental health clinician a minimum of every 30 days.

Mental Health 74 All female prisoners shall be seen by a licensed mental health clinician within five working days of return from a hospital post-partum.

Mental Health 75 A mental health assessment of a prisoner during initial intake shall be completed by mental health staff by the end of the second full day after the prisoner's arrival into ADC.

Mental Health 76 If the initial mental health assessment of a prisoner during initial intake is not performed by licensed mental health staff, the prisoner shall be seen by a mental health clinician within fourteen days of his or her arrival into ADC.

Mental Health 77 Mental health treatment plans shall be updated a minimum of every 90 days for MH-3A, MH-4, and MH-5 prisoners, and a minimum of every 12 months for all other MH-3 prisoners.

Mental Health 78 All mental health treatment plan updates shall be done after a face-to-face clinical encounter between the prisoner and the mental health provider or mental health clinician.

Mental Health 79 If a prisoner's mental health treatment plan includes psychotropic medication, the mental health provider shall indicate in each progress note that he or she has reviewed the treatment plan.

Mental Health 80 MH-3A prisoners shall be seen a minimum of every 30 days by a mental health clinician.

Mental Health 81 MH-3A prisoners who are prescribed psychotropic medications shall be seen a minimum of every 90 days by a mental health provider.

Mental Health 82 MH-3B prisoners shall be seen a minimum of every 90 days by a mental health clinician.

Mental Health 83 MH-3B prisoners who are prescribed psychotropic medications shall be seen a minimum of every 180 days by a mental health provider. MH-3B prisoners who are prescribed psychotropic medications for psychotic disorders, bipolar disorder, or major depression shall be seen by a mental health provider a minimum of every 90 days.

Mental Health 84 MH-3C prisoners shall be seen a minimum of every 180 days by a mental health provider.

Mental Health 85 MH-3D prisoners shall be seen by a mental health provider within 30 days of discontinuing medications.

Mental Health 86 MH-3D prisoners shall be seen a minimum of every 90 days by a mental health clinician for a minimum of six months after discontinuing medication.

Mental Health 87 MH-4 prisoners shall be seen by a mental health clinician for a 1:1 session a minimum of every 30 days.

Mental Health 88 MH-4 prisoners who are prescribed psychotropic medications shall be seen by a mental health provider a minimum of every 90 days.

Mental Health 89 MH-5 prisoners shall be seen by a mental health clinician for a 1:1 session a minimum of every seven days.

Mental Health 90 MH-5 prisoners who are prescribed psychotropic medications, shall be seen by a mental health provider a minimum of every 30 days.

Mental Health 91 MH-5 prisoners who are actively psychotic or actively suicidal shall be seen by a mental health clinician or mental health provider daily.

Mental Health 92 MH-3 and above prisoners who are housed in maximum custody shall be seen by a mental health clinician for a 1:1 or group session a minimum of every 30 days.

Mental Health 93 Mental health staff (not to include LPNs) shall make weekly rounds on all MH-3 and above prisoners who are housed in maximum custody.

Mental Health 94 All prisoners on a suicide or mental health watch shall be seen daily by a licensed mental health clinician or, on weekends or holidays, by a registered nurse.

Mental Health 95 Only licensed mental health staff may remove a prisoner from a suicide or mental health watch. Any prisoner discontinued from a suicide or mental health watch shall be seen by a mental health provider, mental health clinician, or psychiatric registered nurse between 24 and 72 hours after discontinuation, between seven and ten days after discontinuation, and between 21 and 24 days after discontinuation of the watch.

Mental Health 96 A reentry/discharge plan shall be established no later than 30 days prior to release from ADC for all prisoners who are MH-3 or above.

Mental Health 97 A mental health provider treating a prisoner via telepsychiatry shall be provided, in advance of the telepsychiatry session, the prisoner's intake assessment, most recent mental health treatment plan, laboratory reports (if applicable), physician orders, problem list, and progress notes from the prisoner's two most recent contacts with a mental health provider.

Mental Health 98 Mental health HNRs shall be responded to within the timeframes set forth in the Mental Health Technical Manual (MHTM) (rev. 4/18/14), Chapter 2, Section 5.0.

Mental Health 99 Peer reviews shall be conducted as set forth in the MHTM (rev. 4/18/14), Chapter 1, Section 3.0.

Dental 100 Prisoners on the routine dental care list will not be removed from the list if they are seen for urgent care or pain appointments that do not resolve their routine care issues or needs.

Dental 101 Dental assistants will take inmate histories and vital signs and dental radiographs (as ordered) by the Dentist.

Dental 102 Routine dental care wait times will be no more than 90 days from the date the HNR was received.

Dental 103 Urgent dental care wait times, as determined by the contracted vendor, shall be no more than 72 hours from the date the HNR was received.

JUDICIAL DECISIONS ON EXHAUSTION

Plaintiff Earl Farmer[186] is a prisoner in the custody of the Idaho Department of Correction (IDOC) alleged that Defendants failed to protect him from physical and sexual assault by other inmates and were deliberately indifferent to his mental health. *Compl.*, Dkt. 3. Farmer asserted civil rights claims under § 1983, as well as unidentified state law claims. The court states in pertinent part:

"The defendant bears the ultimate burden of proving failure to exhaust[187]. If the defendant initially shows that (1) an available administrative remedy existed and (2) the prisoner failed to exhaust that remedy, then the burden of production shifts to the plaintiff to bring forth evidence "showing that there is something in his particular case that made the existing and generally available administrative remedies effectively unavailable to him." *Albino, 747 F.3d at 1172*. Confusing or contradictory information given to a prisoner is relevant to the question "of whether relief was, as a practical matter, 'available.'" *Brown, 422 F.3d at 937*. Administrative remedies will be deemed unavailable and exhaustion excused if the inmate had no way of knowing the prison's grievance procedure, if the prison improperly processed an inmate's grievance, if prison officials misinformed an inmate regarding grievance procedures, if the inmate "did not have access to the necessary grievance forms within the prison's time limits for filing the grievance," or if prison staff took any other similar actions that interfered with an inmate's efforts to exhaust. *Albino, 747 F.3d at 1173*.

If a prisoner has failed to exhaust available administrative remedies, the appropriate remedy is dismissal without prejudice.[188]

B. Grievance Procedure

Idaho has adopted a grievance procedure for inmates in its custody. *Whittington Aff.* ÷ 3, Dkt. 18-3. The IDOC grievance procedure consists of a three-step process: (1) the inmate seeks an informal resolution of the matter by completing an Offender Concern Form; (2) the inmate completes a Grievance Form if informal resolution cannot be accomplished; and (3) the inmate appeals any unfavourable response to the grievance. *Id.* ÷ ÷ 5-8. Once all three steps are completed, the offender grievance process is exhausted. *Id.* ÷ 9.

As an inmate incarcerated by the Idaho Department of Corrections, the Offender Grievance Process has been available to Famer. *Id.* ÷ 4; *Grievance and Informal Resolution Procedure for Offenders*, Dkt. 18-4. Farmer fully exhausted two grievances by completing all three steps: Grievance II 130001139 and Grievance II 140001240. *Whitting Aff.* ÷ 11. Grievance II 130001139 concerned the Prison Rape Elimination Act. *Id.* ÷ 13. In Grievance II 140001240, Farmer complained on November 17, 2014, after this suit was filed, that the IDOC and Corizon refused to provide him a parole plan for mental health aftercare (after his release) due to cost. *Id.* ÷ 14. In particular, he wanted the IDOC and Corizon to provide him mental health assistance after his release. *Id.* Farmer also filed a third grievance, which he apparently did not fully complete: Grievance II 130001073. In this last Grievance, Farmer requested counselling or therapy from an outside specialist, but that grievance did not allege that he was denied adequate mental health care due to cost. *Id.* ÷ 12. Farmer concedes that he received six additional counselling sessions as a result of the grievance. *Id.*; *Compl.* at 15, Dkt. 3.

C. Farmer's Failure to Exhaust Administrative Remedies

The record demonstrates that Farmer did not exhaust his administrative remedies through the grievance process any of the allegation raised in his Complaint. In his Complaint, Farmer alleges that Corizon was deliberately indifferent to his mental health when it did not follow the standards as provided for in Corizon's contract with the IDOC. *Compl.*, p. 6, Dkt. 3. He alleges that he requested to have mental health counselling, but his request was refused due to budgetary concerns. *Id.* Farmer further alleges that Corizon does not provide him needed mental health care because it only has one psychologist and no psychiatrist on staff. *Id.* at 6-7. In addition, Farmer alleges that his mental health issues have not been properly diagnosed by a competent licensed mental health professional, and that he has not been placed on a mental health program or pathway that fits his needs. *Id.* at 7. Because he allegedly received inadequate medical care, Farmer claims, he was placed in a living environment where he was physically attacked by another inmate in January 2014. *Id.*

Yet, Farmer never filed a grievance alleging that: (1) Corizon did not follow the mental health standards as provided for in its contract with the IDOC; (2) his mental health care was inadequate due to staffing; (3) his mental health issues have not been properly diagnosed by a competent mental health professional; (4) he has not been placed on a mental health program or pathway that fits his needs; and (5) due to inadequate mental health care, he was placed in a living environment where he was physically assaulted by another inmate in January 2014. *Whittington Aff.* ÷ 15. Because Farmer did not raise any of these specific issues contained in his Complaint in a grievance, the claims in his Complaint are unexhausted and must be dismissed. *Woodford,* 548 U.S. at 85.

Farmer, however, argues that (1) Grievance II-130001073 includes the issues in the Complaint; (2) Grievance II-140001240 is "a continuation" of Grievance II-130001073; (3) Defendant Shell Wamble-Fisher did not allow his Concern Forms or Grievances to be processed between January 2013 and late 2014; and (4) Prison Rape Elimination Act ("PREA") claims do not need to be addressed through the grievance process. *Pl.'s Resp.*, Dkt. 21. The Court disagrees with each of these arguments and will address each in turn.

First, Grievance II-130001073, filed September 9, 2013, does not address the issues raised in the Complaint. Rather, with this grievance, Farmer requested counselling from an outside specialist. This grievance was granted at the Level II response, and Farmer received six outside counselling sessions. But Farmer's contends in his Complaint that he was denied counselling sessions beyond the six sessions provided in response to this Grievance. In other words, this Grievance 1240 did not raise the same issues as those raised in the Complaint..

SECOND, GRIEVANCE 1240 IS NOT A CONTINUATION OF GRIEVANCE II-130001073, AS FARMER CONTENDS. IN GRIEVANCE 1073, FARMER COMPLAINED THAT THE IDOC AND CORIZON REFUSED TO PROVIDE HIM A PLAN FOR MENTAL HEALTH CARE *AFTER* HIS RELEASE FROM PRISON BECAUSE OF COST. WHETHER ADDITIONAL CARE SHOULD HAVE BEEN PROVIDED *WHILE* FARMER REMAINED IN PRISON, WHICH IS WHAT FARMER CONTENDS IN HIS COMPLAINT, IS AN ENTIRELY DIFFERENT ISSUE FROM WHETHER FARMER SHOULD RECEIVE CARE *AFTER* HIS RELEASE, WHILE HE IS ON PAROLE. MOREOVER, THE IDAHO GRIEVANCE POLICY REQUIRES THAT EACH GRIEVANCE ADDRESS ONLY A SINGLE ISSUE AND THERE CANNOT BE "CONTINUING" GRIEVANCES. *GRIEVANCE AND INFORMAL RESOLUTION PROCEDURE FOR OFFENDERS*, P. 9, DKT. 18.

However, even if Grievance 1073 did arguably encompass the allegations in Farmer's Complaint, it was not filed until after the Complaint was filed, and therefore Farmer did not exhaust his administrative remedies prior to initiating this action[189] If Corizon did not know about the specific problem, they could not attempt to remedy it.

Third, there is no evidence that Wamble-Fisher denied Farmer access to the grievance process. The only evidence Farmer provides is a series of documents that appear to come from an unrelated whistle-blower case; Farmer argues that these documents demonstrate Wamble-Fisher's lack of credibility and propensity to alter documents. But these documents do nothing to show that Wamble-Fisher somehow impeded *Farmer's* access to the grievance process. Indeed, the fact that Farmer filed five concern forms and grievances in 2013, and two more in 2014 belies his allegations that Wamble-Fisher prevented him from filing a grievance during this same time frame. Farmer does not explain how he filed these five concern forms or grievance but failed to file a single grievance raising the same concerns raised in his Complaint.

However, even assuming that Farmer's allegations were true, it would not matter because Farmer did not have to go through Wamble-Fisher to file a grievance. The Idaho Grievance Policy makes clear that if a staff member does not respond to an Offender Concern Form within seven days, the inmate can elect to submit another Offender Concern Form to another staff member or use the grievance process. *Grievance and Informal Resolution Procedure for Offenders*, p. 3. Dkt. 18. So, if Wamble-Fisher ignored or impeded Farmer's concern forms or delayed the grievance process as Farmer alleges, he could have simply bypassed that step and filed a grievance in a lockbox that is provided for all inmates to use for confidential offender/grievance/appeal forms. *Id.*, p. 6.

Finally, several problems exist with Farmer's argument that his claim qualifies as a "PREA" claim and thus does not need to be exhausted. Congress enacted the PREA to address the problem of rape in prison by creating national standards to prevent, detect, and respond to prison rape.[190] Neither Farmer's deliberate indifference claim at issue here nor any of the grievances he filed in 2013 and 2014 raise concerns about sexual abuse or prison rape (which he contends occurred in 1997); instead, his claims and grievances involve issues with access to mental health counselling. Thus, it is not clear that Farmer's claim would qualify as a PLRA. Indeed, it is questionable that PREA even creates a private cause of action that can be brought by an individual plaintiff.[191] Finally, many courts have held that the PREA's reporting requirements do not supersede the PLRA's exhaustion requirements[192] In sum, Farmer was required to exhaust his administrative remedies before filing suit but failed to so. Accordingly, the Court will grant Corizon's motion for summary judgment."

Jason Keel[193], a former inmate at the Miami Correctional Facility ("Miami"), brought this action on May 2, 2014, pursuant to *42 U.S.C. § 1983*. (DE #1.) The court states:

"At all relevant times, and pursuant to Indiana Department of Correction ("IDOC") policy, Miami has an Offender Grievance Process under which an inmate can grieve a broad range of issues related to their conditions of confinement. (DE #34-1, Ex. A 7; Ex. B.) All inmates are made aware of the grievance process during orientation and a copy of the process is available in the law library. (Ex. A 7; Ex. B.) The process begins with the inmate attempting to resolve the matter informally with staff. (Ex. A 9.) If the issue cannot be resolved informally, the inmate must file a formal grievance within 10 days of the underlying incident. (*Id.* 9; Ex. B.) If the grievance is not resolved to the inmate's satisfaction, he must file an appeal within

10 working days of the grievance response. (*Id.* 8; Ex. B.) The grievance manager reviews the appeal and submits a response. (*Id.* 7; Ex. B.) An inmate has not fully exhausted the Offender Grievance Process until he completes all three steps of the process and receives a response from the Department's Offender Grievance Manager. (*Id.* 10; Ex. B.) Moreover, exhausting the grievance procedure requires timely pursuing each step of the informal and formal process. (*Id.*)

On October 21, 2013, Keel filed Grievance No. 79052, complaining about the medical care he received from Dr. Kream, Dr. Loveridge and Nurse Shalala. (DE #46 at 11.) He fully exhausted that grievance on December 18, 2013. (*Id.* at 6.) According to the grievance records kept and maintained at Miami, Keel has initiated three (3) grievances in 2014 that have been fully exhausted: Grievance Numbers 81396, 81760 and 82172 (Ex. A, 11; Ex. C.) In Grievance No. 81396, Keel complained about prison staff losing his property in conjunction with a move to the infirmary. (Ex. A 12; Ex. C.) This grievance was not fully exhausted until May 22, 2014. (*Id.*) In Grievance No. 81760, he complained about his medical care, including being in continuous pain and not being able to exercise. (*Id.*) Notably, this grievance complained about Dr. Mandaret, not Dr. Mitcheff. It was not fully exhausted until June 3, 2014. (*Id.*) In Grievance No. 82172, he complained about not being able to obtain information from the state medical licensing board. (*Id.*) This grievance was not fully exhausted until May 29, 2014. (*Id.*)

Pursuant to the Prison Litigation Reform Act ("PLRA"), prisoners are prohibited from bringing an action in federal court with respect to prison conditions "until such administrative remedies as are available are exhausted." *42 U.S.C. § 1997e(a)*. An inmate must exhaust before bringing his lawsuit, and efforts to exhaust while the case is pending do not satisfy *42 U.S.C. § 1997e(a)*.[194] For exhaustion purposes, an inmate is deemed to have "brought" the action on the date when his complaint is tendered for mailing. *Ford, 362 F.3d at 400.*

The failure to exhaust is an affirmative defence on which the defendant bears the burden of proof[195]. The U.S. Court of Appeals for the Seventh Circuit has taken a "strict compliance approach to exhaustion." *Dole, 438 F.3d at 809.* Thus, "[t]o exhaust remedies, a prisoner must file complaints and appeals in the place, and at the time, the prison's administrative rules require."[196] "[A] prisoner who does not properly take each step within the administrative process has failed to exhaust state remedies." *Id. at 1024.*

Here, Dr. Mitcheff argues that Keel did not properly exhaust his administrative remedies before filing suit. As outlined above, the record reflects that Keel exhausted three grievances in 2014 and none were related to Mr. Mitcheff's March 2014 treatment of his hand.

Keel nevertheless maintains that he exhausted his administrative remedies by pointing to a grievance he filed on October 21, 2013. (DE #46 at 6.) However, that grievance was filed four months before Dr. Mitcheff allegedly denied him medical treatment for his hand. In addition, that October 2013 grievance did not relate to Dr. Mitcheff's treatment of Keel's hand. Thus, the October 2013 grievance is insufficient to demonstrate that Keel exhausted his administrative remedies for his claims against Dr. Mitcheff in this case. Therefore, the undisputed facts show that Keel did not exhaust his administrative remedies regarding his claims that Dr. Mitcheff denied him medical treatment for his hand in March 2014 and beyond."

William R. Tubbs[197] ("Plaintiff") is an inmate of the Arkansas Department of Correction ("ADC") and he alleges the named Defendants exhibited deliberate indifference toward his serious medical needs. (Doc. No. 52.) The court states:

"The Prison Litigation Reform Act (PLRA) requires an inmate to exhaust prison grievance procedures before filing suit in federal court.[198] Exhaustion under the PLRA is mandatory. *Jones, 549 U.S. at 211.* "[T]o properly exhaust administrative remedies, prisoners must 'complete the administrative review process in accordance with the applicable procedural rules,' rules that are defined not by the PLRA, but by the prison grievance process itself." *Id., 549 U.S. at 218* (quoting *Woodford v. Ngo, 548 U.S. 81, 88, 126 S. Ct. 2378, 165 L. Ed. 2d 368 (2006))*. Compliance with a prison's grievance procedures is, therefore, all that is required by the PLRA to properly exhaust. *Id.* Thus, the question of whether an inmate has properly exhausted administrative remedies will depend on the specifics of that particular prison's grievance policy. *See Id.* Plaintiff's claims are governed by Administrative Directive 12-16. (Doc. No. 169-1 at 3.) An inmate who believes he has been wronged is first required to file an informal resolution. (*Id.* at 7-10.) If the inmate is unsatisfied with the outcome of the informal resolution, he may proceed to the formal grievance procedure which entitles him to a response, first from the appropriate medical personnel, and then, if desired, from the ADC Deputy Director. (*Id.* at 10-14.) Inmates must be specific as to their issues and any personnel involved. (*Id.* at 7.)

The record shows Plaintiff exhausted eight grievances during the time period relevant to this suit. (Doc. No. 169-1 at 2.) Defendants state none of these grievances properly exhausted any claims against Defendants Morgan, Pevey, or Corizon, LLC. I agree. Neither Morgan nor Corizon, LLC is explicitly referenced in the eight grievances. Plaintiff only names "Pevey" in grievance CU-13-2065. (*Id.* at 45.) Defendants state this is not a reference to Defendant Pevey, who is a nurse, but rather an ADC Garment Factory Supervisor of the same name. (Doc. No. 169 at 4 n.1.) A review of CU-13-2065 supports their assertion. Plaintiff states he sought permission from

Glover and "Pevey", his garment factory supervisors, "not to come back to P.M. work do (sic) to my pain." (Doc. No. 169-1 at 45.)

With respect to Defendant Bland, only grievance CU-13-2064 exhausts relevant claims against her. (*Id.* at 41.) These claims relate to a July 23, 2013, encounter where Plaintiff complained of severe pain but was allegedly not given sufficient pain medication. (*Id.*) Defendant Bland was also referenced in CU-13-01226, but no actual claim was stated against her. (*Id.* at 35.) Rather, this grievance stated Defendant Esaw had not provided Plaintiff with a cane which Bland had previously authorized. (*Id.*)

Based on the foregoing, I recommend Defendants Morgan, Pevey, and Corizon, LLC be dismissed for Plaintiff's failure to exhaust administrative remedies. Additionally, any claims against Defendant Bland which do not arise from the July 23, 2013, encounter should also be dismissed on this basis."

Harold Davey Cassell[199] ("Plaintiff") is an inmate of the Arkansas Department of Correction ("ADC"). He alleges that Corizon, LLC and Correct Care Solutions, LLC ("Defendants") have exhibited deliberate indifference to his serious medical needs. (Doc. No. 1.) Specifically, Plaintiff suffers from Hepatitis-C and contends that Defendants failed to treat his condition with the drugs Victrelis and Incivek when both were approved by the Food and Drug Administration in 2011. (*Id.* at ¶12-15.) He claims Defendants were also deliberately indifferent when they failed to administer the drugs Olysio and Savaldi, which were approved in 2013. (*Id.* at ¶23-26.) Defendants have now motioned for summary judgment (Doc. No. 27) and Plaintiff has responded (Doc. No. 32).

The Prison Litigation Reform Act (PLRA) requires an inmate to exhaust prison grievance procedures before filing suit in federal court.

Exhaustion under the PLRA is mandatory. *Jones, 549 U.S. at 211.* "[T]o properly exhaust administrative remedies, prisoners must 'complete the administrative review process in accordance with the applicable procedural rules,' rules that are defined not by the PLRA, but by the prison grievance process itself." *Id., 549 U.S. at 218* (quoting *Woodford v. Ngo, 548 U.S. 81, 88, 126 S. Ct. 2378, 165 L. Ed. 2d 368 (2006))*. Compliance with a prison's grievance procedures is, therefore, all that is required by the PLRA to properly exhaust. *Id.* Thus, the question as to whether an inmate has properly exhausted administrative remedies will depend on the specifics of that particular prison's grievance policy. *See Id.*

Here, Plaintiff's claims are governed by Administrative Directives 12-16 and 14-16. The relevant procedures for medical grievances are consistent across both directives, which require an inmate who believes he has been wronged to file an informal resolution. (Doc. No. 28-2 at 5-6.) If the inmate is unsatisfied with the outcome of the informal resolution, he may proceed to the formal grievance procedure which entitles him to a response, first from the Health Service Administrator, and then, if desired, from an ADC Deputy, Chief Deputy, or Assistant Director. (*Id.* at 8-11.) Inmates must be specific as to their issues and any personnel involved. (*Id.* at 5-6.)

Defendants state that Correct Care Solutions did not begin their contract with the ADC until January 1, 2014. (Doc. No. 29 at 9.) Plaintiff does not appear to dispute this assertion. From January 1, 2014, until this suit was filed on October 30, 2014, Plaintiff filed thirteen medical grievances. (Doc. No. 28-4 at 1-2.) After review of these grievances, I conclude Plaintiff failed to properly exhaust the claims which he now brings against Correct Care Solutions. Notably, none of the grievances makes any reference to Victrelis, Incivek, Olysio, or Savaldi, the drugs which Plaintiff now alleges should have been administered to him. Instead, the grievances raise various issues which are not relevant to this case: (1) CU-14-00162 complained of anal bleeding, possibly related to haemorrhoids, and alleged that the medication prescribed for this ailment had been ineffective; (2) CU-14-00255 complained that non-party Lasonya Griswold found no need for a medical follow-up despite a diagnostic result indicating that Plaintiff's platelet levels had dropped; (3) CU-14-00477, CU-14-00536, and CU-14-00803 each complain about non-party Laura Morgan's failure to adhere to ADC grievance policy; (4) CU-14-00804 complains that Plaintiff was not afforded an opportunity to discuss the results of a colonoscopy with medical staff; (5) CU-14-00805 and CU-14-00850 allege that Correct Care Solutions and unit medical staff denied him a follow-up with an outside specialist to discuss various medications which that specialist had prescribed; (6) CU-14-00932 and CU-14-01045 allege that non-party Dana Peyton was untruthful in her responses to Plaintiff's earlier grievances; (7) CU-14-01514 asks for the results of a blood test; and (8) CU-14-01515 complains that he has not received boots which medical staff indicated would be prescribed for him. (Doc. No. 28-3 at 4-45.)

For his part, Plaintiff argues that some of the medical conditions rose in the grievances, most notably the anal bleeding, are "extraheptic manifestations" and therefore related to Plaintiff's Hepatitis-C. (Doc. No. 32-3 ¶¶2-3, 7-8.) Accepting this argument as true, Plaintiff still failed to raise the issues which underlie this case, namely whether Correct Care Solutions was deliberately indifferent in failing to prescribe certain drugs to combat his Hepatitis-C. Plaintiff also contends that those grievances which raise issues of inadequate procedure are indicative of an effort by Correct Care Solutions to "cause external impediment" and "deny prisoners due process to the grievance procedure." (*Id.* ¶¶5-6.) These arguments are unsupported by any substantive evidence. Moreover, even if prison staff failed to respond adequately or truthfully to Plaintiff's grievances, there is no indication that anyone prevented Plaintiff from grieving and exhausting the claims he raises in this suit. Finally, Plaintiff states that he apprised Correct Care Solutions of his situation by way of a letter sent by his counsel to the Regional Director. (Doc. No. 32-3 at 36.) This communication was not part of the official grievance procedure, however, and cannot substitute for a properly exhausted grievance.

Based on the foregoing, I recommend that Defendant Correct Care Solutions be dismissed for failure to exhaust administrative remedies.

PLAINTIFF [201] FILED HIS COMPLAINT ON OCTOBER 28, 2014. HE CONTENDS THAT, AFTER UNDERGOING A NECK SURGERY IN OCTOBER 2013, SOMETHING IN HIS NECK "SNAPPED," AND THEREAFTER HE SUFFERED CONTINUOUS PAIN. HE ASSERTS THAT THE MEDICAL PROVIDERS AT THE PRISON--DEFENDANTS DR. MURRAY YOUNG AND NURSE PRACTITIONER WILLIAM POULSON, WHO WORK FOR CORIZON, LLC --HAVE REFUSED TO GIVE HIM PROPER DIAGNOSES AND TREATMENTS AFTER THAT DATE.

IN MARCH 2014, PLAINTIFF SIGNED FORMS GIVING PERMISSION FOR INMATE REPRESENTATIVES IN AN ONGOING CLASS ACTION LAWSUIT TO DISCUSS HIS MEDICAL ISSUES WITH IDAHO DEPARTMENT OF CORRECTION (IDOC) MEDICAL SERVICES ADMINISTRATOR RONA SIEGERT AND OTHERS AT STATUS MEETINGS WHERE THE MONITORING OF THE PROVISION OF MEDICAL SERVICES IS DISCUSSED AMONG IDOC OFFICIALS, CORIZON OFFICIALS, INMATES, LAWYERS, AND OTHER INTERESTED REPRESENTATIVES. THE PERMISSION FORM STATES:

I understand that this form is not a substitute for a . . . grievance form. . . . I am also still required to follow the concern/grievance process if I want to grieve this issue.

(Plaintiff's Exhibit, Dkt. 17-2, p. 1.)

On October 6, 2014, Plaintiff filed a grievance on the same medical issues, which was denied. On November 5, 2014, he filed an appeal, but his appeal form was returned because the handwriting was partially illegible, and he resubmitted it. The response was returned to Plaintiff on November 12, 2014. However, Plaintiff filed his Complaint in this matter on October 28, 2014, before the appeal was completed.

3. IDOC Grievance Process

The IDOC has a simple grievance process, consisting of three stages. First, an inmate with a concern must seek resolution of the problem by filling out an offender concern form, addressed to a staff person capable of resolving the issue. If the issue cannot be resolved through the use of a concern form, the inmate must then file a grievance form. The grievance is then resolved by a Level 1 Initial Response, which is reviewed by a Level 2 Reviewing Authority Response, and then returned to the inmate. If the grievance did not resolve the issue satisfactorily, the inmate must file an appeal, which is reviewed and decided by a Level 3 Appellate Authority Response. When all three of these steps--concern form, grievance form, and grievance appeal-- are completed, the administrative grievance process is exhausted. (Affidavit of Jill Whittington, Dkt. 13-3.) The procedure requires that the grievance and appeal forms be handwritten legibly; if they are not, they are returned to the inmate with instructions to make the writing legible. (IDOC Grievance Procedures, Dkt. 13-4, p. 10.)

4. Discussion and Conclusion

The law is clear that (1) the particular prison grievance procedures must be followed as specified in the prison's written policies; and (2) a claim cannot be included in a civil rights complaint unless it was exhausted before the time it is first included in the lawsuit. Here, Plaintiff attempted to informally resolve his problem by taking it to the class action medical monitoring meeting. However, nowhere does Plaintiff point to any procedures that state that this method is an acceptable alternative to filing a prison grievance, or to any official statement by a prison administrator letting him know that he had satisfied the grievance procedures in an alternative manner and had the green light to file a lawsuit without using the established grievance procedures. The form itself contradicts his argument.

The fact that completion of the grievance process was delayed because Plaintiff submitted a partially illegible appeal was his own fault, and he was simply required to rewrite it and resubmit it, which he did. A legible appeal is a reasonable requirement, because prison officials cannot know of the problem if they cannot read the grievance appeal. However, after resubmitting the grievance appeal in a legible form, Plaintiff then was required to wait for a response from his grievance appeal before filing his lawsuit, which he did not do.

One of the reasons prisoners must follow the internal grievance system is to allow prison officials to fix problems internally, without the need for filing a costly, time-consuming lawsuit. Another reason is to provide them with legal notice, so that a lawsuit can be filed if officials do not fix the problem at the grievance or appeal stage. Yet another reason is to aid prisoners in the rehabilitative process--they are in prison for failing to follow society's rules, and the sooner they understand the importance of rules and learn how to follow them with exactness, the better able they are to function within the prison society and, if released, within the society at large. The bottom line is that "before" means before.

The undisputed material facts show Plaintiff did not follow the rules of administrative exhaustion. The United States Supreme Court has clarified that exactness in following the administrative exhaustion rules is required. No adequate excuse for failing to follow the rules is evident from the record. The Court rejects Plaintiff's argument that he did not first present his claim in his lawsuit at the time he first presented the lawsuit for filing--simply because his lawsuit was "conditionally" filed by the Clerk of Court. It is not the category in which the Clerk accepted and filed the lawsuit that is at issue, but the fact that Plaintiff presented it for filing at that time.

Therefore, this case must be dismissed without prejudice. However, because Plaintiff is still within the statute of limitations period on his more current lack-of-care claims, he may re-file his lawsuit immediately, based upon any completed grievances, and so Defendants' procedural victory may be short-lived.

Plaintiff [202] asserts that he is entitled to summary judgment on Defendants' affirmative defence that Plaintiff failed to exhaust his available administrative remedies. He argues that he was excused from the exhaustion requirement under the plain terms of Arizona Department of Corrections (ADC) Department Order 802.01, § 1.8, which Plaintiff asserts exempts emergency complaints from the formal grievance procedure. Plaintiff further asserts that, even though he was not required to exhaust administrative remedies, he did exhaust his administrative remedies by following the ADC's grievance procedure.

Defendants respond that "Plaintiff's conclusory statements citing to D.O. 802 are not enough to prove that his specific medical complaints constituted an 'emergency condition' within the meaning of D.O. 802" and that Plaintiff has failed to present evidence demonstrating that his prostate cancer presented an emergency medical condition under D.O. 802. Defendants further assert that D.O. 802.01, §1.8 does not obviate an inmate's obligation to exhaust the ADC's grievance and appeals procedures in the event of an emergency, but "simply allows an inmate to bring an emergency to the attention of staff, by any available means, rather than to rely on the written grievance procedure to alert staff to an emergency." (Doc. 137 at 6.)

Defendants next assert that the Grievance Appeal Response signed by Director Ryan on February 28, 2014 does not show that Plaintiff exhausted his administrative remedies because "Plaintiff does not provide any documents that were submitted by him as part of the grievance process related to the Grievance Appeal Response signed by Director Ryan on February 28, 2014, or any additional documents related to the other grievances submitted by Plaintiff." (Doc. 140 at 5.)

Under the Prison Litigation Reform Act, a prisoner must exhaust "available" administrative remedies before filing an action in federal court.[203] The prisoner must complete the administrative review process in accordance with the applicable rules.[204] Exhaustion is required for all suits about prison life[205], regardless of the type of relief offered through the administrative process.[206]

The defendant bears the initial burden to show that there was an available administrative remedy and that the prisoner did not exhaust it.[207] Once that showing is made, the burden shifts to the prisoner, who must either demonstrate that he, in fact, exhausted administrative remedies or "come forward with evidence showing that there is something in his particular case that made the existing and generally available administrative remedies effectively unavailable to him." *Albino, 747 F.3d at 1172*. The ultimate burden, however, rests with the defendant. *Id.* Summary judgment is appropriate if the undisputed evidence, viewed in the light most favourable to the prisoner, shows a failure to exhaust. *Id. at 1166, 1168*; *see Fed. R. Civ. P. 56(a)*.

If summary judgment is denied, disputed factual questions relevant to exhaustion should be decided by the judge; a plaintiff is not entitled to a jury trial on the issue of exhaustion. *Albino, 747 F.3d at 1170-71.* But if a court finds that the prisoner exhausted administrative remedies, that administrative remedies were not available, or that the failure to exhaust administrative remedies should be excused, the case proceeds to the merits. *Id. at 1171.*

ADC Department Order 802.06 outlines the formal inmate medical grievance process. (Doc. 113-2 at 5.) An inmate may appeal a response to a formal inmate medical grievance to the Director. (*Id.* at 6.) The decision of the Director for medical grievance appeals is final and constitutes exhaustion of all remedies for inmate medical grievances within ADC. (*Id.* at 7.) Section 802.01 entitled "General Information" provides, in part, that "[i]nmates are not required to use the formal Inmate Grievance Procedures to submit a verbal or written emergency complaint." (*Id.* at 3.) An emergency is defined as "a condition which, if processed through the normal grievance time frames, would subject the inmate to substantial risk of medical harm, personal injury or cause other serious and irreparable harm." (*Id.*) The Department Order further provides that "[a]ny emergency complaint received by staff shall be immediately evaluated through the chain of command to determine whether it is an emergency as defined in 1.8.1 of this section and requires immediate response outside of the Inmate Grievance Procedure time frames."

Plaintiff argues that he was excused from the exhaustion requirement under the plain terms of ADC Department Order 802.01, § 1.8, which provides that "[i]nmates are not required to use the formal Inmate Grievance Procedures to submit a verbal or written emergency complaint." The emergency complaint procedure, however, is not a model of clarity. Section 1.8 clearly states that inmates are not required to use the formal grievance process in the case of an emergency, but provides no further information as to exhaustion of remedies in the case of an emergency. The consequences of this ambiguity are on display in this case.

The Court is unconvinced by Defendants' argument that an inmate must still follow the formal grievance process even after submitting an emergency complaint. It is Defendants who are able to define the grievance process and how administrative remedies are exhausted and, thus, any ambiguity in their policy should be construed in favour of Plaintiff. *See Woodford, 548 U.S. at 90* (proper exhaustion requires using all steps that the agency holds out, and doing so properly).

Plaintiff provides a "consultation request" signed by Dr. Kessler, which states that Plaintiff told him that it was important to establish care with a urologist for treatment of his prostate cancer. (Doc. 25-9 at 1.) He argues that this evidence shows he orally pursued treatment for his prostate cancer and, therefore, was exempt from the formal administrative grievance process. Defendants argue that Plaintiff has not shown that his condition constituted an emergency within the meaning of Section 1.8.1, which provides that an emergency is "a condition which, if processed through the normal grievance time frames, would subject the inmate to substantial risk of medical harm, personal injury or cause other serious and irreparable harm." The Department Order, however, does not state who decides which conditions are "medical emergencies" or what happens when, after evaluation, a complaint is deemed to not constitute an emergency.

Despite the substantial ambiguity in the emergency complaint grievance process, Plaintiff is entitled to summary judgment on Defendants' exhaustion of administrative remedies affirmative defence because the uncontroverted evidence shows that he exhausted his claims to the Director's level. Plaintiff provides a January 13, 2014 response from Director Ryan responding to Plaintiff's request for "immediate and thorough treatment for [his] cancer or immediate release to get treatment by a competent doctor due to the life threatening nature of [his] cancer." (Doc. 114-2 at 1-2.) Defendants state that Plaintiff has failed to show that he exhausted his claims in this action because he did not provide any of the grievance documents that led **to Director Ryan's final decision with his Motion for Summary Judgment. But Defendants point to nothing in their policy requiring Plaintiff to name every defendant or explicitly set forth his legal claims in his grievances.**208Plaintiff provides evidence that he exhausted his claims related to the fact that he was not being provided immediate and thorough treatment for his cancer. Defendants have not met their burden of demonstrating that Plaintiff did not exhaust his claims, and cannot shift the burden to Plaintiff by claiming that Plaintiff has not produced enough evidence to demonstrate that he did exhaust. See Albino, 747 F.3d at 1172 (the ultimate burden of proof as to exhaustion remains with the defendant). Plaintiff has provided unrebutted evidence that he exhausted his administrative remedies, and thus, the Court finds that Plaintiff is entitled to summary judgment on the exhaustion defence.

Plaintiff's209 claims for relief and the court states "Defendants argue this case is due to be dismissed because prior to filing this cause of action Plaintiff failed to properly exhaust an administrative remedy available to him through the prison system's medical care provider, Corizon, Inc., prior to initiation of this case. Doc. No. 13, at 12-15. Defendants base their exhaustion defense on Plaintiff's failure to submit any medical grievances regarding the claims presented. Id., Sagers-Copeland Affidavit. In addition, Defendants maintain, and the evidentiary materials, including Plaintiff's medical records, indicate that Plaintiff received appropriate medical treatment during the time relevant to the matters alleged in the instant complaint. See Doc. No. 13, Ellis, Sagers-Copeland, & Guice Affidavits & Exh. A. On April

13, 2015, the court provided Plaintiff an opportunity to file a response to Defendants' report in which he was advised to "specifically address Defendants' argument that he [] failed to exhaust his available administrative remedies as required by 42 U.S.C. ~ 1997e(a) of the Prison Litigation Reform Act ('PLRA')." Doc. No. 17 at 1 (footnote omitted). On May 5, 2015, the court granted Plaintiff's request for additional time to file his response. Doc. No. 19. Plaintiff has filed no response within the time allowed by the court.

"[A]n exhaustion defense . . . is not ordinarily the proper subject for a summary judgment [motion]; instead, it should be raised in a motion to dismiss, or be treated as such if raised in a motion for summary judgment."[210] Therefore, the court will treat Defendants' report as a motion to dismiss.

In addressing the requirements of *42 U.S.C. § 1997e* regarding exhaustion, the Eleventh Circuit has recognized that "[t]he plain language of th[is] statute makes exhaustion a precondition to filing an action in federal court."[211] This means that "until such administrative remedies as are available are exhausted," a prisoner is precluded from filing suit in federal court.

The court has, therefore, determined that "the question of exhaustion under the PLRA [is] a 'threshold matter' that [federal courts must] address before considering the merits of the case.[212] The court will "resolve this issue first." *Id.*

When deciding whether a prisoner has exhausted his remedies, the court should first consider the plaintiff's and the defendants' versions of the facts, and if they conflict, take the plaintiff's version of the facts as true. "If in that light, the defendant is entitled to have the complaint dismissed for failure to exhaust administrative remedies, it must be dismissed."[213] If the complaint is not subject to dismissal at this step, then the court should make "specific findings in order to resolve the disputed factual issues related to exhaustion." *Id. (citing Bryant, 530 F.3d at 1373-74, 1376).Myles, 476 F. App'x at 366.*

A district courtmay resolve disputed factual issues where necessary to the disposition of a motion to dismiss for failure to exhaust [without a hearing]. *See [Turner, 541 F.3d at 1082].* The judge properly may consider facts outside of the pleadings to resolve a factual dispute as to exhaustion where doing so does not decide the merits, and the parties have a sufficient opportunity to develop the record. *Bryant, 530 F.3d at 1376.Trias, 587 F. App'x at 535.*

Upon review of the complaint, Defendants' special report, and the evidentiary materials filed in support thereof, the court concludes that Defendants' motion to dismiss is due to be granted.

II. DISCUSSION

Plaintiff challenges the adequacy of medical care received at the Staton Correctional Facility for a heart condition. *Doc. No. 1.* In response to the complaint, Defendants deny that they provided Plaintiff with constitutionally inadequate medical care and argue this case is subject to dismissal because Plaintiff failed to exhaust the administrative remedy provided by the institutional medical care provider prior to filing this complaint as required by the Prison Litigation Reform Act, *42 U.S.C. § 1997e(a). Doc. No. 13, Sagers-Copeland Affidavit, Exh. A.* As explained, federal law directs this court to treat Defendants' response as a motion to dismiss for failure to exhaust an administrative remedy and allows the court to look beyond the pleadings to relevant evidentiary materials in deciding the issue of proper exhaustion. *Bryant, 530 F.3d at 1375.*

The Prison Litigation Reform Act compels exhaustion of available administrative remedies before a prisoner can seek relief in federal court on a ˜ *1983* complaint. Specifically, *42 U.S.C.* ˜ *1997e(a)* states that "[n]o action shall be brought with respect to prison conditions under *section 1983* of this title, or any other Federal law, by a prisoner confined in any jail, prison, or other correctional facility until such administrative remedies as are available are exhausted." "Congress has provided in ˜ *1997e(a)* that an inmate must exhaust irrespective of the forms of relief sought and offered through administrative remedies."[214] "[T]he PLRA's exhaustion requirement applies to all inmate suits about prison life, whether they involve general circumstances or particular episodes, and whether they allege excessive force or some other wrong." [215] Exhaustion of all available administrative remedies is a precondition to litigation and a federal court cannot waive the exhaustion requirement.[216] Moreover, "the PLRA exhaustion requirement requires proper exhaustion." *Id. at 93*.

Proper exhaustion demands compliance with an agency's deadlines and other critical procedural rules [as a precondition to filing suit in federal court] because no adjudicative system can function effectively without imposing some orderly structure on the courts of its proceedings . . . . Construing ˜ *1997e(a)* to require proper exhaustion . . . fits with the general scheme of the PLRA, whereas [a contrary] interpretation [allowing an inmate to bring suit in federal court once administrative remedies are no longer available] would turn that provision into a largely useless appendage.

Id. at 90-91, 93. The Supreme Court reasoned that because proper exhaustion of administrative remedies is necessary an inmate cannot "satisfy the Prison Litigation Reform Act's exhaustion requirement . . . . by filing an untimely or otherwise procedurally defective administrative grievance or appeal[,]" or by effectively bypassing the administrative process simply by waiting until the grievance procedure is no longer available to her. *Id. at 83-84*; *Bryant, 530 F3d at 1378* (quoting *Johnson v. Meadows, 418 F3d 1152, 1158 (11th Cir. 2005)* ("To exhaust administrative remedies in accordance with the PLRA, prisoners must 'properly take each step within the administrative process.'"); *Johnson, 418 F.3d at 1157* (inmate who files an untimely grievance or spurns the administrative process until it is no longer available fails to satisfy the exhaustion requirement of the PLRA); *Higginbottom, 223 F.3d at 1261* (inmate's belief that administrative procedures are futile or needless does not excuse the exhaustion requirement). "The only facts pertinent to determining whether a prisoner has satisfied the PLRA's exhaustion requirement are those that existed when he filed his original complaint."[217]

The record is undisputed that the health care provider for the Alabama Department of Corrections provides a grievance procedure for inmate complaints related to the provision of medical treatment. *Doc. No. 13, Sagers-Copeland Affidavit*. Defendants submitted evidence which reflects that when inmates are processed into the custody of the Alabama Department of Corrections they are informed of the process and procedure for obtaining medical care and medication and are also educated about the availability of the medical grievance process whereby they may voice complaints regarding any medical treatment sought or received during their incarceration. *Id.* Inmate grievance forms are available to inmates at Staton to submit a grievance related to the provision of health care, inmate grievances are answered within approximately ten days of receipt of the grievance, and the inmate grievance form provides information about how an inmate may appeal the response he receives to his initial inmate grievance. *Id.* A written response to a formal grievance appeal is provided in approximately ten days of receipt. *Id.* Inmates are provided with a copy of the completed grievance and/or grievance appeal containing the health service administrator's response. *Id.* Defendants state

Plaintiff has submitted no medical grievances or medical grievance appeals of any kind nor did he ever request any assistance in notifying the Staton medical staff of any complaints, concerns or grievances he possessed relative to the medical care he has received at Staton. *Id.; Exh. A*.

The court granted Plaintiff an opportunity to respond to the exhaustion defence raised by Defendants in their motion to dismiss but he did not do so. *Doc. No. 17*. The court, therefore, finds that a grievance system is available at Staton for Plaintiff's claims, but he failed to exhaust the administrative remedy available to him. Plaintiff does not dispute his failure to submit any grievances related to the provision of his medical care at Staton, and the unrefuted record before the court demonstrates he failed to properly exhaust an administrative remedy available to him at Staton regarding his allegation of inadequate medical care prior to seeking federal relief, a precondition to proceeding in this court on his claims. Any grievances filed after initiation of this federal cause of action have no bearing on Plaintiff's proper exhaustion of the administrative remedy provided by the facility's medical provider. *Terry, 491 F. App'x at 83*.

Accordingly, Defendants' motion seeking dismissal for Plaintiff's failure to exhaust available administrative remedies should be granted, and such dismissal should be without prejudice. *See Ngo, 548 U.S. at 87-94; Bryant, 530 F.3d at 1374-1375* (dismissal for failure to exhaust an administrative remedy when the remedy remains available is not an adjudication of the merits and is without prejudice); *Woodford, 548 U.S. at 87-94*.

Colen's [218] claims stem from medical care related to an injury he sustained in 2010, when he allegedly broke his foot playing basketball. When he was first evaluated by defendant Rogers, he was diagnosed with a sprain and given an ace bandage. [R. 13, PgID 82].

Over the next two and a half years, he continually kited various medical providers for assistance for increasing pain in his foot, swelling, and new pain in his knee, but he was told that his pain was either a sprain or simply arthritis and he was given minimal care. X-rays taken much later revealed knee deterioration requiring replacement, arthritis, and an old foot fracture that had not healed properly. [*Id.*, PgID 83-92]. Colen had knee replacement surgery in 2014, but continued to experience foot pain that remained untreated. [*Id.* 93-94].

Colen's amended complaint alleges that the MDOC Defendants' conduct violated his *Eighth* and *Fourteenth Amendment* rights, and constituted intentional infliction of emotional distress and gross negligence. [R. 13]. The MDOC Defendants now move for summary judgment, alleging that Colen failed to properly exhaust his administrative remedies. This Court disagrees.

III. ANALYSIS

Colen filed five arguably relevant grievances between April and October 2013, but the Court will address only one because it is dispositive. In grievance ARF-13-09-2586-12d1, Colen addressed the entire medical history that gave rise to his amended complaint, stating, "I am continually being denied medical treatment for the injury sustained on my foot where I have broken bones and torn ligaments which have worsened over the last two years." [*Id.*, PgID 323]. He emphasized, "I have tried unsuccessfully to resolve my condition with the Health care staff, and the Adrian Administration. Nothing is being done to correct my foot, knee and leg, and I am in excruciating pain." [*Id.*]. He alleged that "Health Care and the Adrian Staff are being deliberately indifferent by purposefully ignoring my request [to see a specialist and receive injections] and ailment." [*Id.*].

MDOC resolved this grievance on its merits. [*Id.*, PgID 320-22]. In fact, MDOC informed Colen on January 31, 2014, that its denial of this Step III grievance represented an exhaustion of his administrative remedies. [*Id.*, PgID 320].

Nonetheless, the MDOC defendants now argue that grievance ARF-13-09-2586-12d1 was not properly exhausted because Colen did not specify the names of those involved, in violation of MDOC policy. [R. 40, PgID 297]. But, that argument was rejected by the Sixth Circuit in *Reed-Bey v. Pramstaller, 603 F.3d 322, 324-25 (6th Cir. 2010)*, because the state failed to follow its own procedural rule requiring the prisoner to name those involved, and instead decided the otherwise defaulted claims on the merits. "When prison officials decline to enforce their own procedural requirements and opt to consider otherwise-defaulted claims on the merits, so as a general rule will we." *Id. at 325*.

Since MDOC decided grievance ARF-13-09-2586-12d1 on its merits, in disregard for the requirement that he name all those involved, this Court should decide the merits of his claims, too.

JUDICIAL DECISIONS ON PRSON HEALTHCARE[219]

On July 9, 2014, Plaintiff Kevin Mitchell[220], who is represented by counsel, filed a Complaint in the Maricopa County Superior Court. On August 5, 2014, Defendants Corizon Health, Inc. (Corizon) and the State of Arizona removed the action to this Court. On August 13, 2014, Defendants Corizon and State of Arizona filed an Answer to the Complaint. In a November 3, 2014 Order, the Court dismissed the Complaint because Plaintiff had failed to state a claim. The Court gave Plaintiff 30 days to file an amended complaint that cured the deficiencies identified in the Order.

On December 3, 2014, Plaintiff filed his First Amended Complaint (Doc. 7). The Court will dismiss Plaintiff's federal claim against Talboy, order Corizon to answer Plaintiff's federal claim against it, and order Corizon, the State, and Talboy to answer Plaintiff's state law claim.

II. First Amended Complaint

In his two-count First Amended Complaint, Plaintiff sues Corizon, Registered Nurse Patricia Talboy, and the State. Plaintiff demands a jury trial and seeks monetary damages, pre- and post-judgment interest, and his attorneys' fees and costs.

Plaintiff contends that the State has entered into contracts, first with one private health care provider and then with Corizon, to administer and provide health care to Arizona inmates. Plaintiff contends that the State and Corizon have been unwilling to appropriately staff Arizona prisons with sufficient and competent health care providers.

Plaintiff contends that the State's health care delivery system lacks an adequate tracking and management system to ensure that inmates with chronic conditions, such as Plaintiff, receive "competent and appropriate medication administrations." Plaintiff claims that the State is deliberately indifferent to inmates' health care needs because it has failed to hire, manage, supervise, control, maintain, operate and oversee health care at the prison where Plaintiff is confined. Plaintiff asserts that the State, to the detriment of inmates, has consciously and deliberately breached its duty of care by awarding health care contracts to the lowest bidder. Plaintiff contends that Corizon, to the detriment of inmates, has placed its own profits ahead of inmate safety by deliberately refusing to properly staff Arizona prisons and by hiring inexperienced nurses and other healthcare providers.

Plaintiff alleges that he is confined at the Arizona State Prison Complex-Lewis (ASPC-Lewis), suffers from Type 1 diabetes, and requires insulin injections. He claims that in August 2012, a nurse (who was employed by Corizon's predecessor) contaminated ASPC-Lewis's insulin supply and exposed Plaintiff and other inmates to life-threatening diseases such as hepatitis and the human immunodeficiency virus (HIV). He asserts that the State and Corizon were deliberately indifferent to the serious medical needs of inmates because they failed to take appropriate measure to ensure that future contamination would not occur.

Plaintiff alleges that on January 5, 2014, Defendant Talboy, who had less than six months' experience as a nurse, failed to follow proper, specific, well-established insulin delivery protocols and exposed Plaintiff and other inmates to bloodborne pathogens such as hepatitis and HIV. Plaintiff asserts that Talboy used a needle to stick each patient's finger to check their blood sugar levels, cleaned the needle with alcohol, and then used the needle to draw insulin from a vial and administer insulin to the patient. Plaintiff states that this contaminated the insulin that remained in the vial and that Talboy repeated this process with five inmates. Plaintiff claims Corizon, with deliberate indifference to inmate healthcare, used the same contaminated insulin vials the following day, thereby contaminating more inmates. Plaintiff alleges that "Defendants" failed to inform Plaintiff of his exposure until January 7, 2014. At that point, Defendants provided Plaintiff with multiple preventative treatments and prescribed medications.

Plaintiff alleges that Talboy was deliberately indifferent when she chose to ignore specific, standard, and well-established nursing protocols. Plaintiff also alleges that the State and Corizon tasked Talboy with the responsibility of administering insulin without first ensuring that Talboy was properly trained to do so and that Corizon was deliberately indifferent because it placed profits over patient safety when it hired an inexperienced nurse and failed to properly train and supervise her.

Plaintiff contends that he has been needlessly exposed to potentially dangerous diseases, received potentially dangerous injections, was forced to undergo medical testing and treatment, and has suffered pain, discomfort, anxiety, and extreme emotional distress after being told he had been exposed to potentially deadly viruses.

In Count One, Plaintiff alleges a claim under *42 U.S.C. § 1983* against Corizon and Talboy. Plaintiff contends that both Defendants were deliberately indifferent to Plaintiff's needs and unnecessarily exposed Plaintiff to deadly diseases by giving him a contaminated injection. Plaintiff claims that Corizon had a policy of placing profits ahead of inmate needs, failed to properly staff the prison with competent healthcare providers, and hired new and inexperienced providers, such as Talboy, who could be paid less than more experienced and qualified nurses. Plaintiff also alleges that Corizon had a policy and custom of understaffing Arizona prisons to reduce costs and increase profits, at the expense of providing quality healthcare to inmates. Plaintiff contends that Corizon's decision and custom to improperly staff and train its nurses violated Plaintiff's *Eighth* and *Fourteenth Amendment* rights.

Plaintiff also asserts that Talboy's violation of specific, standard and well-established nursing protocols was more than neglect because "Nursing 101 establishes that dirty needles should never be placed into insulin that would then be subsequently used for other inmates/patients." Plaintiff contends that Talboy's actions exhibited a "complete and total disregard for inmate safety" and deliberate indifference to the serious medical needs of the inmates she treated.

In Count Two, Plaintiff alleges a state law "negligence and willful or wanton conduct" claim against the State, Corizon, and Talboy.

Plaintiff's allegations do not support a claim that Talboy was acting with deliberate indifference when she contaminated the insulin vial and injected Plaintiff. Talboy may have been negligent, grossly negligent, or committed medical malpractice, but none of these rise to the level of deliberate indifference. Thus, the Court will dismiss Plaintiff's deliberate indifference claim against Talboy.

In his Complaint, Larsgard [221] set forth two counts for relief: a medical-care claim under the *Eighth Amendment* (Count I) and a gross negligence/negligence claim under state law (Count II) (Doc. 1 ¶36-56). Larsgard alleged that when he entered the ADC in April 2012, he had a pre-existing spinal condition that caused chronic, severe pain, muscle spasms, and seizures (*id.* 14). He claimed that in December 2012, he suffered a seizure, fell out of bed, and injured his neck and spine (*id.* ¶14-15). The fall caused further nerve damage and left him partially paralyzed, and shortly thereafter, he underwent emergency surgery on his neck and spine (*id.* ¶15-17, 19). According to Larsgard, following surgery, the treating neurosurgeon, Dr. Ali A. Baaj, recommended that Larsgard see a pain-management specialist for his chronic, severe pain and receive follow-up treatment within 30 days, including MRI/CT scans, so that a neurologist could evaluate whether his spine was properly healing and the bolts in his neck and spine remained in place (*id.* 20). Larsgard alleged that despite these recommendations, he was not returned for follow up until late July 2013, six months later, and at that time, the x-rays and MRI imagings had not yet been taken (*id.* 21).

Larsgard averred that as of the date of his Complaint (August 23, 2013), he had not seen a pain management specialist for his chronic, severe pain (*id.* 22). He further averred that his medication is ineffective and inadequate to control his seizures, muscle spasms, and neuropathic pain, and the medication that is provided is routinely out of supply or discontinued for non-medical reasons (*id.*).

Larsgard seeks injunctive and declaratory relief for the alleged *Eighth Amendment* violation ((*id.* ¶40-46). Specifically, he requests an injunction against Corizon to (1) perform the requisite imaging studies of his neck and spine; (2) refer him to a pain management specialist; and (3) timely administer his medications (Doc. 39 at 2). Larsgard also seeks compensatory and punitive damages and costs (Doc. 1 ¶57-60).

In 2009, Larsgard underwent posterior cervical fusion surgery in Germany (Doc. 33, Def.'s Statement of Facts (DSOF 2); Doc. 40, Pl.'s Controverting Statement of Facts (PCSF) 2). In December 2012, while in ADC custody, Larsgard fainted in his cell and hit the back of his head, which caused upper extremity paresthesia and neck pain (DSOF 3; PCSF 3). This pain was exacerbated on January 1, 2013, when Larsgard turned his head and lost consciousness (*id.*). He was taken to the emergency room and later admitted to the University of Arizona Medical Center, where x-rays revealed a C6 fracture (Doc. 40, Pl.'s Statement of Facts (PSOF) 1 & Ex. 1 (Doc. 40-1 at 5)). Larsgard underwent a posterior cervical fusion and laminectomy performed by Dr. Ali Baaj (DSOF 3; PCSF 3). Thereafter, on January 11, 2013, Larsgard was transferred to a rehabilitation facility, and Dr. Baaj prescribed a list of medications, which included narcotics and benzodiazepines (DSOF 4; PCSF 4). Upon Larsgard's discharge, Dr. Baaj recommended he return for follow up 3 weeks after surgery, and a typical follow up is usually 2-3 weeks after surgery, then again at 3 months, and then at 6 months (PCSF 8).

Larsgard received pain management treatment post-surgery at the Medical Center and the rehabilitation facility; however, the parties dispute whether this pain management treatment was with a specialist (PSOF 2; Doc. 42 2). Dr. Baaj has recommended pain management treatment since the surgery (PSOF 2; Doc. 42 at 2).

On February 11, 2013, after Larsgard's return to prison, prison physician Dr. Kevin Lewis noted that in addition to the MS Contin (morphine) prescribed by Dr. Baaj for post-surgical pain, Larsgard had a history of taking a high dose of opioids from 2009 (DSOF 6; PCSF 6). Prior to his incarceration, Larsgard was treated by a physician in Norway for chronic, severe neck pain (PSOF 3). The Norwegian physician tried alternative treatments and pain medications but determined that a combination of opioids and benzodiazepines was the only effective treatment for Larsgard's severe pain (*id.*).

On March 4, 2013, Corizon assumed care and treatment of Larsgard when it replaced Wexford as the contracted entity with the State of Arizona to provide healthcare services to inmates (Doc. 32 at 4 n. 1).

Corizon states that Dr. Lewis attempted to wean Larsgard off of the high dose opioid analgesics and, in an April 2013 medical note, documented that Larsgard "is highly resistant to wean off opioid analgesics. My goal is gradual wean to lowest dose to maintain function" (DSOF 7). Larsgard states that Dr. Lewis advised him that Corizon ordered Dr. Lewis to discontinue morphine pain medication per its policy (PCSF 7). Larsgard states that his pain medication regularly "ran out," which caused him to suffer severe bouts of pain (*id.*).

Larsgard was not seen by Dr. Baaj for follow up until July 26, 2013 (DSOF 8; PCSF 8). At this appointment, Dr. Baaj noted that Larsgard had no post-op x-rays so he ordered that an x-ray and imagings "be performed immediately" and that a disk with the results be mailed to the hospital neurosurgery clinic (*id.*). He also ordered that Larsgard follow up with the neurosurgery clinic in 6 months for a cervical spine CT (DSOF 8).

On August 20, 2013, Larsgard saw prison Nurse Practitioner Richard Unger (DSOF 9). The medical record from this encounter reflects that the two discussed pain management and that Larsgard stated he felt his pain was under control with morphine sulfate (MS Contin) but he requested diazepam (Valium) for muscle spasms (Doc. 33, Ex. L (Doc. 33-1 at 23)). Larsgard was already on diazepam, but Unger increased the dosage and also submitted a consult request for a CT of the cervical spine in 6 months per Dr. Baaj's request (*id.*; PCSF 9). Thereafter, a "Utilization Management" physician reviewed Larsgard's medication history, determined that his medication combination with diazepam was a dangerous combination, and ordered that the dosage be reduced to prevent any adverse reaction (Doc. 40, Ex. 10 (Doc. 40-10 at 1)).

Defendant states that on August 22, 2013, x-rays were ordered for Larsgard's cervical spine, as requested by Dr. Baaj (DSOF 10).

On September 11, 2013, Larsgard met with Dr. Dimitri Catsaros at the prison; Dr. Catsaros ordered that the MS Contin (morphine) be continued (DSOF 11; PCSF 11).

On October 18, 2013, an MRI and CT of the cervical and thoracic spine were performed (DSOF 12; PCSF 12). The results, received on December 3, 2013, stated that the hospital chose not to perform the x-rays; that the CT scan showed a healed and aligned cervical spine and an unremarkable thoracic spine; and that metal placements in the spine created distortion and prevented an accurate MRI reading (DSOF 12).

On November 26, 2013, a neurological consult was ordered; the consult request was approved on December 5, 2013 by the Medical Director (DSOF 13).

On March 10, 2014, pursuant to the consult request, Larsgard saw Dr. Baaj, and Larsgard reported that his pain symptoms had improved (*id.*; PCSF 13). Dr. Baaj determined Larsgard had full range of motion of the neck without pain and "shows good alignment"; he noted that the C6/7 fracture had healed; he recommended pain management; and he noted that no further follow up was needed (DSOF 13 (in part) & Doc. 33, Ex. Q (Doc. 33-1 at 37)).

On March 18, 2014, Larsgard reported that he suffered a seizure and complained of neck pain; he was transferred to the University of Arizona Medical Center emergency facility (DSOF 14; PCSF 14).

New CT scans were taken of Larsgard's head and neck, and all findings were negative for abnormalities (*id.*).

On March 27, 2014, Larsgard was transferred to the ADC Yuma facility (DSOF 15; PCSF 15).

On April 3, 2014, Larsgard saw Dr. Elijah Jordan at the prison (DSOF 16; PCSF 16 (in part)). Dr. Jordan advised Larsgard that it was time to wean off of the narcotic medications and replace them with non-narcotic medication; Larsgard was apprehensive to changes because his medications were at a comfortable level, although he also complained of neck pain (*id.*). Dr. Jordan ordered a tapering down of MS Contin over a period of 4 weeks and started prescriptions for Effexor and Baclofen, which act as muscle relaxants (DSOF 17).

In PCSF 16, Larsgard asserts that Effexor is known to induce seizures, and asks the Court to take judicial notice of a website, "PDRhealth" at www.pdrhealth.com/drugs/effexor, and the information provided therein about Effexor. Corizon objects generally to PCSF 16; however, it is not clear whether it objects to this specific statement and website citation (Doc. 42 11). Nonetheless, the Court will not consider the asserted fact because there is no statement or affidavit from a physician to support that Effexor was contraindicated for Larsgard due to the risk of seizures or any of the other risks listed[222].

On April 10, 2014, Larsgard saw Dr. Jordan again, at which time Larsgard reported that he did not feel well and he had suffered fainting episodes, and he had vomited after taking his medications (DSOF 18; PCSF 18). Dr. Jordan discontinued Effexor and replaced it with Depakote (DSOF 18). A couple days later, Dr. Jordan also prescribed Pamelor (DSOF 19). On April 16, 2014, a nurse notified Dr. Jordan that Larsgard refused his daily dosage of Depakote due to intolerance of the medication; therefore, Dr. Jordan continued tapering down the narcotics and discontinued Depakote and replaced it with Alph Lipoic Acid--a non-narcotic medication (*id.*). Dr. Jordan also prepared a consult request for a physician for pain management (*id.*).

On May 7, 2014, Larsgard again saw Dr. Jordan; Larsgard complained of pain, discomfort, and hypoglycemic symptoms (DSOF 20). The medical note from this appointment reflects that Dr. Jordan planned to prescribe Lyrica (Doc. 42, Ex. 2). The Lyrica prescription was submitted and, shortly thereafter, Dr. Jordan received the alternative recommendation of an equivalent medication, Neurontin (also known as Gabapentin) (Doc. 47 2). On May 21, 2014, Dr. Jordan prescribed Neurontin/Gabapentin, a non-narcotic medication, as a replacement pain medication in lieu of Lyrica (*id.*; PCSF 19).

Meanwhile, on May 15, 2014, the request for an off-site consultation for pain management was approved (DSOF 22).

On May 21, 2014, Larsgard complained of an increased heart rate and appeared to have possible tachycardia issues, so the Pamelor prescription was immediately discontinued (DSOF 21). But Larsgard was administered Pamelor for two more days (PCSF 21).

On May 23, 2014, Larsgard began receiving the Neurontin/Gabapentin; however, it provided no relief (Doc. 40, Ex. 8, Larsgard Decl. 20 (Doc. 40-8 at 4)).

On June 3, 2014, pursuant to the off-site consultation request, Dr. Kevin S. Ladin, a physician board certified in pain medicine and physical medicine and rehabilitation, examined Larsgard (Doc. 40, Ex. 7, Ladin Decl. ¶1-2 (Doc. 40-7 at 1)). In his subsequent report, Dr. Ladin stated that Larsgard has suffered significant nerve damage and has incomplete spinal cord injury, resulting in a legitimate pain syndrome (*id.*, Ex. 6 at 6 (Doc. 40-6 at 6)). Dr. Ladin recommended that Larsgard receive treatment for chronic pain management consistent with the underlying pathophysiology of his pain, including a combination of a neuropathic analgesic medication like Neurontin combined with an antidepressant like Cymbalta (*id.*). He further stated that topical analgesics like Baclofen can be utilized as a muscle relaxant (*id.*). Dr. Laden recommended against the use of opioid or benzodiazepine medications because they have not been shown to be beneficial in neuropathic pain syndrome and have a high risk of dependency and addiction (*id.*). Dr. Ladin also opined that it is medically necessary for Larsgard to be treated by a pain management specialist with experience in spinal cord care and physical medicine (*id.*, Ex. 7, Ladin Decl. ¶3-4 (Doc. 40-7 at [*16] 1-2)).

In its reply, Corizon argues that Dr. Ladin's declaration is deficient because it was not timely disclosed, it is improper as an expert opinion, and it is without foundation (Doc. 41 at 3-4). To the extent Corizon objects to Dr. Ladin's declaration, the objection is overruled. The declaration satisfies *Rule 56(c)(4)*, and prior disclosure of a declaration used to oppose summary judgment is not required. *See* n. 5. Also, Corizon is incorrect that it is not clear whether Dr. Ladin is referring to Larsgard's past or present treatment needs; his recommendations include no use of the past tense and are clearly referring to present treatment needs (Doc. 40-7 at 1-2).

In early June 2014, a prescription for Cymbalta was written; however, for reasons unknown, Larsgard did not receive this medication (Doc. 43 4; Doc. 47 4). Dr. Jordan has prescribed an equivalent medication, Prozac, which Larsgard is currently taking (Doc. 47 4).

On July 9, 2014, Baclofen was discontinued (Doc. 43 1; Doc. 47 1). Corizon states that it was discontinued at Larsgard's request (Doc. 47 1). Larsgard disputes that he ever requested to be taken off Baclofen as it was the only muscle spasm pain relief he was taking (Doc. 48 2).

Accordingly, Corizon fails to meet its initial summary judgment burden on this portion of Larsgard's claim.

In light of the material factual dispute regarding whether there is deliberate indifference to Larsgard's current serious medical need, the Motion for Summary Judgment will be denied.

Plaintiff Edward Allen Moore ("Moore")[223] seeks monetary damages against Defendant Corizon, LLC ("Corizon") for failing to perform a tooth extraction for eight months. (ECF No. 3, ¶2). Moore claims that he experienced "excruciating dental pain during the month of July 2009 while incarcerated at the [Missouri Department of Corrections ("MDOC")] Northeast Correctional Center." (ECF No. 3, ¶11). Moore submitted a Medical Services Request ("MSR") and a dentist determined that Moore needed a tooth extracted. (*Id.*). Moore asserts that he unnecessarily suffered between July 2009 until his tooth was extracted on March 3, 2010. (*Id.*). Moore filed a Petition, alleging claims under *Section 1983* (Count I), breach of contract (Count II), negligence per se (Count III), and negligence (Count IV). Corizon removed the Petition and has moved to dismiss all of Corizon's claims.

The Court holds that Moore has sufficiently alleged violation of an unconstitutional policy that resulted in injury. Moore alleges in his Petition that Corizon's agents failed to adhere to MDOC policies to ensure timely access to health services. Moore further alleges he was injured in that he waited eight (8) months for a tooth extraction. The Court finds that Moore has sufficiently alleged that Corizon's violation of MDOC policies resulted in an unreasonable delay in receiving a tooth extraction. Therefore, the Court denies Corizon's motion to dismiss with respect to Count I.

Records indicate Plaintiff [224] was issued a medical script allowing him to possess a cane on September 18, 2012. (Doc. No. 169-2 at 15.) This script was reissued after his transfer to the Cummins Unit. (*Id.* at 19-20.) Plaintiff alleges Defendant Esaw failed to timely fill this script, however. (Doc. No. 52 at 8.)

Plaintiff alleges Defendant Bland was deliberately indifferent to his serious medical needs when, after an encounter on July 23, 2013, she did not increase his dose of pain medication. (Doc. No. 52 at 8-9.) Instead, Defendant Bland recommended he continue his present dose until he could confer with a physician - Dr. Schock - in **the next five to ten days. (Doc. No. 169-3 at 2.) Defendants have provided the affidavit of Dr. Floss who opines this decision was medically appropriate. (Doc. No. 169-2 at 2.) I find this sufficient to recommend dismissal of this claim against Defendant Bland. Here, Plaintiff has failed to provide any substantive evidence or argument which would call Defendant Bland's decision into serious question. If he has such evidence, he may include it in his objections to this recommendation.**[225]

According to Plaintiff[226], while he was housed at MRF from 1997 to May 27, 2008, he repeatedly complained to healthcare services about pain in his lower back, right wrist and hand, left knee, and shoulders. Plaintiff was eventually diagnosed with "Juvenile Arthritis Disease" and given prescriptions for the nonsteroidal anti-inflammatory drugs (NSAIDs) Naprosyn and Motrin to treat his pain. (*Id.* at 4.) On May 27, 2008, he was transferred to KCF, where he continued to receive NSAIDs, including Motrin, Mobic, Lodine, and Tylenol, as well as a sleeping agent, Elavil. After his transfer, he repeatedly complained to healthcare services about pain that was radiating into his neck, shoulders, lower back, pelvis, thighs, legs, knees, and feet. On November 12, 2009, Defendants Nevai, Kingsbury, Paneque, and Gulick, acting on behalf of the MDOC, allegedly entered into a contract with Corizon and Aetna for the provision of medical care to Michigan prisoners. On December 21, 2010, Nurse Rogers diagnosed Plaintiff with "Paget's Disease," but refused to treat it due to "non-medical [reasons and budget cuts." (*Id.* at 5.) Plaintiff repeatedly complained to healthcare services about painful symptoms, including sensations of burning, stinging, electrical shocks, being stabbed, as well as numbness and tingling radiating down his buttocks to his feet. (*Id.*)

According to the National Institutes of Health, Paget's disease of the bone "is a disorder that involves abnormal bone destruction and regrowth. This results in deformity of the affected bones[,]" which can cause pain and other symptoms. NIH, National Library of Medicine, HTTPS://WWW.NLM.NIH.GOV/MEDLINEPLUS/ENCY/ARTICLE/000414.HTMHTTPS://WWW.NLM.NIH.GOV/MEDLINEPLUS/ENCY/ARTICLE/000414.HTM (visited August 24, 2015).

On September 8, 2011, Nurse Rogers ordered x-rays of Plaintiff's lower spine. After reviewing the results, the MDOC's radiologist recommended further assessment with an MRI and further "workup" of Plaintiff's Paget's disease. (*Id.*) Plaintiff received an MRI of his spine on October 19, 2011, "without contrast." (*Id.*) The doctor reviewing the results indicated that the report was delayed because "Postcontrast Images" were not authorized. (*Id.*) Nevertheless, the report revealed a number of issues, including "Severe degener[a]tive disk disease," "Moderate Central Canal Stenosis," "Bilateral Neural Foraminal Stenosis," "Broad based Central disk herniation," "Mild Central Stenosis," and possible "Spondylodiskitis." (*Id.* at 5-6.) Plaintiff alleges that Defendant Stieve prevented the physician from providing adequate medical care and management of Plaintiff's pain, and prevented Plaintiff from receiving a MRI with "Post Contrast Images," for budgetary reasons. (*Id.* at 6.)

Plaintiff continued to complain about his symptoms, and on October 25, 2011, Nurse Rogers referred him to the MDOC's Pain Management Committee. On November 2, 2011, Defendant Stieve denied Plaintiff "appropriate" pain medication and a referral to a neurosurgeon, despite the fact that the medication Plaintiff was receiving was not adequate. Plaintiff subsequently filed a "formalized complaint" with Dr. Stieve, Dr. Neri and Nurse Rogers regarding a lack of treatment for his pain, which had become so severe that it was affecting his ability to stand or walk for prolonged periods of time. (*Id.* at 6-7.) On December 20, 2011, Plaintiff filed a grievance against Defendants Stieve, Neri and Rogers for depriving him of adequate medical care and a consultation with a neurosurgeon.

On January 10, 2012, Plaintiff filed a "formalized complaint" with Defendants Stieve, Neri and Rogers, detailing his continuing symptoms and asking to be referred to a specialist for consideration of other treatment options. (*Id.* at 7.) On January 17, 2012, Plaintiff filed a grievance against Defendants Stieve, Neri and Rogers regarding their refusal to provide adequate pain medication or to refer him to a specialist.

On March 13, 2012, Nurse Rogers referred Plaintiff to the MDOC's Pain Management Committee for reevaluation of Dr. Stieve's prior decision. Dr. Stieve denied access to additional medication or a consultation with a neurosurgeon.

Plaintiff met with Nurse Rogers on May 23, 2012, and informed her that the sleeping agent did not relieve his pain and was causing other complications, and that the NSAID pain medication was not effective. Plaintiff asked for an epidural injection. Nurse Rogers decided to discontinue the sleeping agent and told him that she had done all that she could. She referred Plaintiff to Dr. Neri. Plaintiff informed Dr. Neri that the sleeping agent and NSAIDs were not effective. Dr. Neri referred Plaintiff to the MDOC's Pain Management Committee. Once again, on August 29, 2012, Dr. Stieve denied Plaintiff additional pain medication and a consultation [with a neurosurgeon.

A few days later, on September 5, 2012, Plaintiff asked Dr. Neri why Dr. Stieve would prescribe Elavil, knowing that Plaintiff suffers harmful side effects from it (i.e., migraines) and that it did not alleviate Plaintiff's symptoms. Dr. Neri stated that he did not have authority to order a "non-formulary" medication; only Dr. Stieve had that authority. (*Id.* at 9.) Plaintiff asked Dr. Neri for a referral to a neurosurgeon. Dr. Neri stated that Dr. Stieve would not approve such a consultation until Plaintiff could no longer walk. Plaintiff continued to complain, and Dr. Neri left the room and returned with Nurse Rogers. Dr. Neri then performed a prostate examination on Plaintiff in front of Nurse Rogers, which involved "[poking], pushing and squeezing" Plaintiff's prostate gland while asking, "[I]s it coming out yet? It is coming out yet?," until Plaintiff's gland was "empty" and there was a "large" amount of "cloudy" fluid on the floor. (*Id.* at 10.)

Plaintiff felt humiliated by this experience. He asked if that was the proper method for performing a prostate exam, and Dr. Neri stated, "This is the proper way of doing a Prostate Examination, you have to feel how large the gland is, feel for any small bumps on the gland and . . . squeeze the fluid out." (*Id.*) Plaintiff subsequently filed a "formalized complaint" with the MDOC's "Bureau of Health Service" and with Defendants Stieve, Neri and Rogers for being denied pain medication and a consultation with a neurosurgeon, and for being subjected to an "inappropriate" prostate examination. (*Id.*)

On September 17, 2012, during Plaintiff's annual screening, Nurse Rogers stated that: Dr. Stieve "[i]s not going to give Plaintiff narcotic for pain"; "no surgeon is going to tear up Plaintiff's back for Spinal Stenosis"; and that Plaintiff would not receive a consultation with a neurosurgeon until he is not able to move his legs or feet. (*Id.* at 11.) In addition, she stated that "[i]f Plaintiff keeps complaining about [t]he Psychotropic medication, all [Dr. Stieve] is going to give Plaintiff . . . is Aspirin and Anti-Inflammatory (NSAID)." (*Id.*) Nurse Rogers attempted to perform a prostate examination, but Plaintiff refused. Three days later, Plaintiff filed a grievance against Defendants Stieve, Rogers and Neri, complaining that they were ignoring his symptoms and forcing him to take a psychotropic medication (Elavil) that gives him migraine headaches, and a sleeping agent (Pamelor) that does not work.

Plaintiff requested a transfer out of KCF. On April 30, 2013, he was transferred to MCF into the care of Dr. Williams Nelson and Physician Assistant (PA) Barbara Bien (who are not Defendants in this action). The next month, on May 19, he filed a "formalized complaint" with the healthcare unit at MCF, requesting a hot water bottle, a walking cane, and a TENS unit for his "severe and painful neurology symptoms." (*Id.* at 12.) Three days later, he filed a grievance complaining that he was denied a hot water bottle, walking cane, and a TENS unit.

Plaintiff uses the term "Tents Unit," but the Court assumes that Plaintiff is referring to a TENS device, which transmits an electric current through the skin in order to stimulate nerves and provide relief from pain. *See*

HTTP://WWW.WEBMD.COM/PAIN-MANAGEMENT/TC/TRANSCUTANEOUS-ELECTRICAL-NERVE-STIMULATION-TENS-TOPIC-OVERVIEWHTTP://WWW.WEBMD.COM/PAIN-MANAGEMENT/TC/TRANSCUTANEOUS-ELECTRICAL-NERVE-STIMULATION-TENS-TOPIC-OVERVIEW (visited August 24, 2015).

On July 13, 2013, Plaintiff filed a "formalized complaint" with the MDOC's "Bureau of Health Care," requesting the names of all doctors and other medical staff who were involved in making decisions on behalf of the Pain Management Committee. (*Id.*) Eleven days later, he filed a grievance complaining that "Defendants" denied him this information or prevented him from obtaining it. (*Id.*)

At a medical examination on September 9, 2013, Plaintiff was informed by Dr. Nelson that there was no medical reason for Defendant Neri to "milk" Plaintiff's prostate gland, unless Neri needed a sample to check for an infection. (*Id.*)

In December 2013, Plaintiff filed a criminal complaint with the Michigan state police against Defendants Stieve, Neri, Rogers, Laughhunn, Lamb, and Russell. He also filed a grievance complaining that: (1) Director Heyns, along with Corizon and Aetna, approved and implemented a policy of cutting costs that resulted in less effective medical care for Plaintiff; (2) Defendants Stieve, Neri, and Rogers failed to provide an adequate MRI, failed or refused to provide Plaintiff with a consultation with a neurosurgeon, and failed or refused to provide adequate pain medication; and (3) Defendants Stieve, Neri, Rogers, Lamb, and Laughhunn failed or refused to take corrective action in response to Plaintiff's alleged sexual assault (i.e. prostate exam) by Defendant Neri.

In January 2014, Plaintiff received a response to his criminal complaint, indicating that all matters regarding the denial of health care would be referred to the Internal Affairs division of the MDOC, and that division would review Plaintiff's allegations to determine whether a criminal investigation is warranted.

On February 5, 2014, after Plaintiff continued to complain about his "painful neurology symptoms," PA Bien referred Plaintiff to the

MDOC's Pain Management Committee. (*Id.* at 14.) Two weeks later, Dr. Stieve denied Plaintiff additional pain medication and a consultation with a neurosurgeon.

On February 24, 2014, Plaintiff complained to Bien that his pain had spread to the right side of his neck and arms. She referred him to the Pain Management Committee, requesting a MRI of Plaintiff's spine and x-rays of his neck. Plaintiff received x-rays of his spine on February 26, 2014, which revealed "Mild Anterior Spondylosis" of his C5 and C6 vertebrae, "Mild Posterior Spurring" in the C5 vertebra, and "Early Arthritic changes." (*Id.* at 15.) Defendants Stieve and Papendick denied the referral for a MRI, concluding:

Medical necessity is not demonstrated at this time. Even if there was difficulty with the patient[']s back there would be no surgery to induce more pain than the patient already has. No bladder or bowel issues and a regular X-Ray at DWH would give indication if there was significant change in the patient's Lumbar Spine. Finally[,] the patient should have a single visit consult with The [MDOC]'s Physical Therapist, for Home Exercise Program.

(*Id.* at 15.) Defendants Stieve and Papendick subsequently approved a referral for physical therapy.

A week later, Plaintiff filed a grievance complaining that Stieve and Papendick refused to approve a MRI or a referral to a neurosurgeon, and refused to provide additional pain medication or other treatment options until Plaintiff became incontinent.

Plaintiff met with a physical therapist at Duane Waters Hospital on March 19, 2014. The therapist provided exercise recommendations, but indicated that if they did not help within 90 days, then Plaintiff should be taken to a neurosurgeon for surgery, because there was nothing else that could be done.

Plaintiff met with PA Bien on May 29, 2014, regarding his painful symptoms. She recommended a referral to a neurosurgeon and referred Plaintiff to the Pain Management Committee. The next day, Dr. Papendick and Dr. Stieve denied the referral to a neurosurgeon, stating:

a.) Criteria not met; b.) Medical necessity not demonstrated at this time; c.) Medical work not up to date; *and* d.) *Review up to date for guidelines.* (Compl., Page ID#16 (emphasis in original).) On June 4, 2014, Dr. Stieve issued an addendum denying Plaintiff additional pain medication and a referral to a neurosurgeon. Stieve allegedly retaliated against Plaintiff by stating that if Elavil is not helping, Plaintiff should stop taking it. Almost two weeks later, Plaintiff filed a grievance against Defendants Stieve, Neri, Papendick, Corizon, and Aetna complaining that they have a "Blanket Policy" of denying Plaintiff a referral to a neurosurgeon and denying him additional pain medication. (*Id.* at Page ID#17.)

On July 14, 2014, Plaintiff filed a "formalized complaint" with Dr. Nelson, PA Bien, and Defendants Papendick, Stieve, and Corizon regarding new symptoms, including numbness on the left side of Plaintiff's head radiating down the left side of his face along his left temple and eye, as well as dizziness and feeling disoriented. Two weeks later, after Plaintiff continued to complain about his symptoms, he filed a grievance against Nelson, Bien, Papendick, and Stieve, complaining that they were ignoring his new symptoms.

On October 21, 2014, Bien recommended that Plaintiff receive an MRI of his spine. Dr. Papendick rejected the recommendation because the "[c]riteria [are] not met," and "[m]edical necessity [is] not demonstrated," but he approved an electromyograph (EMG) of Plaintiff's lower extremities. (*Id.* at Page ID##17-18.)

On November 3, 2014, Plaintiff filed a grievance against "Defendants et. al," claiming that they removed $10.00 from his prison account in order to discourage him from filing "formalized medical complaints" and grievances. (*Id.* at Page ID#18.) The following day, he filed a grievance against Defendants Nevai, Kingsbury, Paneque and Gulick, claiming that they "knew or should have known" that they put Plaintiff's health at risk by entering into a contract with Corizon and Aetna, who are "nationally recognized and re[k]nown for civil rights violations of deliberate [i]indifferen[ce] to prisoner's medical needs." (*Id.*)

Plaintiff received an electromyograph (EMG) on November 24. The physician performing the test, Dr. Gray Gurden, was not able to obtain a reflex response from Plaintiff's right knee. Plaintiff informed Dr. Gurden of his ongoing pain and other neurological symptoms, including numbness, tingling, and inability to stand and walk for prolonged periods of time. Dr. Gurden responded that he could not diagnose Plaintiff's symptoms, as the MDOC was only paying him to conduct the EMG.

On December 5, 2014, Plaintiff filed a grievance against Corizon and Aetna regarding their alleged failure to "hire, establish and maintain credential[ed] doctors . . . certified in the field of Orthopedic [sic] and Neurology," and their failure to treat Plaintiff's ongoing symptoms resulting from a herniated disk, a bulging disk, spinal stenosis, and Paget's disease. (*Id.* at Page ID#19.) In January 2015, Plaintiff filed a grievance complaining about Dr. Gurden's inability to diagnose Plaintiff's symptoms because the MDOC would only pay for the EMG.

In a supplement to the complaint (docket #5-1), Plaintiff alleges that the EMG showed evidence of "mild sensory peripheral polyneuropathy." (*Id.* at Page ID#71.) Based on these results, PA Bien recommended that Plaintiff be issued Neurontin. On March 18, 2015, Dr. Kerstein reviewed Bien's recommendation and denied the medication. Plaintiff subsequently filed a grievance against Dr. Kerstein.

Plaintiff asserts that he has suffered permanent injury as a result of Defendants' failure to properly diagnose and/or treat his conditions. He is no longer able to stand or walk in an upright position. He is constantly hunched over to his right side and he walks with a limp. He has lost the "refle[x]" muscle in his right knee. (Compl. at Page ID#28.) In addition, he has suffered permanent nerve damage, resulting in pain and numbness in his neck, arms, lower back, legs, pelvis and feet.

Based on the foregoing, Plaintiff asserts a number of legal claims against Defendants under ~ *1983* and state law. For instance, he contends that Defendants retaliated against him in violation of the *First Amendment*, and subjected him to cruel and unusual punishment in violation of the *Eighth Amendment* and the Michigan Constitution.

As relief, Plaintiff seeks a declaratory judgment, damages, and a permanent injunction requiring, among other things, that Plaintiff be taken to a neurosurgeon for further diagnosis and treatment.

Plaintiff[227] names Corizon Incorporated, Registered Nurse Julie Lucek, and Complex Site Manager Elsie Stowell as Defendants in the Complaint. Plaintiff raises two claims for relief.

In Count One, Plaintiff claims his Eighth Amendment rights were violated when he was denied medication and appropriate treatment after knee surgery. Plaintiff states that on July 18, 2013, he had knee surgery for a meniscus tear. Plaintiff was instructed to rest and elevate his knee, ice the operated area for 30 minutes on/30 minutes off during the first two days, take medication as directed, and bear weight on his leg "as tolerated." Plaintiff claims that after returning to ASPC-Winslow, where he was confined at the time, a nurse wrote out a daily activity order that included meals in his living quarters and no school or recreation activities, and issued Plaintiff a pair of crutches. Plaintiff claims that a few hours later he was called to medical to receive medication. Plaintiff informed the officer on duty that he had just had surgery and could not make it to medical on crutches. Plaintiff alleges that Defendant Lucek eventually brought Plaintiff his medication but informed him that he would have to come to medical to pick up his next dose of medication.

Plaintiff states that he was then later called to "medical" to "sign another laid in order terminating the previous order." Plaintiff again informed detention officers that he could not make it to medical. Plaintiff claims that "medical never called Plaintiff to pick up his medication or brought him his medication ever again." Plaintiff claims that "medical" terminated the previous order and stopped his "meals and ice for his swollen knee[,] disregarding the doctor's instructions." Plaintiff alleges that "medical" and Defendant Lucek knew of his need for medication, ice, and meals, but failed to take reasonable measures, and that Defendant Lucek was deliberately indifferent to the doctor's instructions and failed to provide needed treatment to Plaintiff.

In Count Two, Plaintiff claims that he informed Defendant Stowell, through a grievance, that he was not receiving medication, meals, or ice. Plaintiff alleges that Defendant Stowell responded by telling him that the doctor's instructions are recommendations and that "they (medical) can either follow those recommendations or write their own." Plaintiff claims that Defendant Stowell knew of Plaintiff's need for medication, meals, and ice, but failed to respond reasonably. Plaintiff alleges that as a result of Defendant Stowell's failure to order treatment, he suffered unnecessary and wanton infliction of pain.

Plaintiff also alleges that the knee injuries are continuing and that he has been denied a walking cane.

In his Complaint, Plaintiff[228] alleges three counts. Defendants are: (1) Corizon Health, Health Administrator for the Arizona Department of Corrections ("ADOC"); (2) Dr. Sandoval, M.D., doctor for the ADOC at the Arizona State Prison Complex, Aspen Unit, in Phoenix, Arizona; and (3) Dr. Winskie, "psych doctor" at the Arizona State Prison Complex in Tucson, Arizona.

In Count One, Plaintiff alleges that Defendants were deliberately indifferent to Plaintiff's serious medical needs in violation of the Eighth Amendment as follows: From March 2013 to July 2013, "Corizon Health/Dr. Sandoval" neglected Plaintiff's healthcare. When Plaintiff was admitted to the Aspen Medical Men's Treatment Unit, Dr. Sandoval, "with Corizon's knowledge," discontinued a pain shot of Toradol, which had previously been prescribed to Plaintiff. Dr. Sandoval discontinued the shot of Toradol without evaluating Plaintiff and no pain medication was issued to Plaintiff until July 2013. As a result of the discontinuation of Toradol, Plaintiff "was subject to immense pain in [his] neck and back for four months." Dr. Sandoval threatened Plaintiff that if he "pressed the issue" he would be sent to a different location. Because Plaintiff "feared reprisal," he did not put in a health needs request.

In Count Two, Plaintiff alleges that Defendants were deliberately indifferent to Plaintiff's serious medical needs in violation of the Eighth Amendment as follows: Dr. Winskie and Corizon abruptly discontinued Plaintiff's "psych medications" of Seroquel 600mg without stepping Plaintiff down or putting him on something else for several days. As a result, Plaintiff had numerous thoughts of suicide and severe clinical depression on his days without medication.

"Corizon nurses did everything they could to stop the grievance process to include misplacing paperwork."

In Count Three, Plaintiff alleges that Defendants violated his right to access the grievance process without retaliation as follows: Corizon, Dr. Sandoval, and Dr. Winskie colluded to retaliate against Plaintiff if his grievances were to proceed to the highest level. Dr. Sandoval specifically threatened to move Plaintiff from the facility. As a result, Plaintiff was in a state of constant fear of being removed from the facility, which caused him anxiety, depression, and lingering thoughts of suicide.

EXHAUSTION OF REMEDIES SHOULD NOT BE REQUIRED WHEN AUTHORITIES HAVE MADE IT A PRACTICE NOT TO CORRECT PAST CONDITIONS

As a response to the false perception that court were intruding in prison matters Congress enacted PLRA and the mandatory exhaustion provisions. The intent was to afford prison autorities the opportunity to correct constitutional violations. The cases discussed above and the following grievances are an example why prisoners do not have available for them administrative remedies within the meaning of PLRA.

Justice Kagan in Ross v Blake, NO: 15-339 (U.S.Sup.Ct. 2016) stated when prison authorities refuse to exercise their authority to afford relief, there is no available remedy. The above cases and grievances show that there are no available administrative remedies for prisoners as prison authorities refuse to exercise their authority.

CONCLUSION

It is imperative that PLRA be amended to require administrative remedies be both effective and adequate and holding accountable those officials who are involved in the process. Courts should exempt prisoners in states such as Arizona where prison authorities have refused to exercise their authority in past grievances to correct violations. Prison authorities should not be allowed to play fast and loose with the courts by demanding administrative exhaustion when they have made it abundantly clear from their past actions they will not correct constitutional violations absent a court order.

REFERENCES

[1] Justin James Thrasher is a student at the University Of London Post Graduate Laws Programme offered by University College London and Queen Mary University Of London. He graduated with a B.S. in Global Business from Arizona State University and MBA from California Coast University. He has 9 years experience with Public Law and healthcare litigation involving prison officials and is co-founder of the Arizona Transformational Project and has co-authored Reducing Recidivism in Arizona for the Arizona Governor's Recidivism Project Team. He may be contacted at jt135@student.londoninternational.ac.uk and at jjthrasher135@gmail.com

[2] Has his LL.M with Merit from The University of London, University College London and Queen Mary University specializing in Public International Law, European law and Public Law. Tripati has a B.Sc. in Federal Litigation and PhD in International Finance and Business relations. He has 35 years experience in Public Law Litigation, litigation involving fraud upon the courts and corruption of the truth seeking process by state prosecutors and counsel for healthcare providers as well as counsel for prison authorities. He may be contacted at farlaw@msn.com and tripati@sbcglobal.net

[3] In addition to those who have reviewed the research and provided helpful comments we express our sincere thanks and appreciation to Dorothy, Allan, Lisa, Michelle, Christy, Matt, Aradhna, Arvita, Krish, Rob, Glen and Fred for helping us research and type this document.

[4] See "AN INEXPLICABLE DEFORMITY" by ANANT KUMAR TRIPATI. ISBN: (SURESHOTSBOOKS.COM)(Due late 2017)

[5] *See* Moragne v. States Marine Lines, Inc., 398 U.S. 375, 403 (1970) (discussing "desirability that the law furnish a clear guide for the conduct of individuals . . . and the necessity of maintaining public faith in the judiciary as a source of impersonal and reasoned judgments"); *see also* La. ex rel. Francis v. Resweber, 329 U.S. 459, 470 (1947) (Frankfurter, J., concurring) (stating that the problem before the Court "involve[d] the application of standards of fairness and justice broadly conceived . . . . [N]ot the application of merely personal standards but the *impersonal standards* of society which alone *judges* as the Organs of Law are empowered to enforce" (emphasis added)).

[6] . *See* Schiavone v. Fortune, 477 U.S. 21, 27 (1986) (noting that the Court had "rejected an approach that pleading [was] a game of skill in which one misstep [could] be decisive" (citing Conley v. Gibson, 355 U.S. 41, 48 (1957), *abrogated by* Bell Atl. Corp. v. Twombly, 127 S. Ct. 1955, 1968-69 (2007))); Foman v. Davis, 371 U.S. 178, 181 (1962) (stating that it is "entirely contrary to the spirit of the Federal Rules of Civil Procedure for decisions on the merits to be avoided on the basis of . . . mere technicalities").

[7] . *See, e.g.*, Ogden v. San Juan County, 32 F.3d 452, 455 (10th Cir. 1994) ("[A]appellant's *pro se* status does not excuse the obligation of any litigant to comply with the fundamental requirements of the Federal Rules of Civil and Appellate Procedure."); King v. Atiyeh, 814 F.2d 565, 567 (9th Cir. 1987) ("Pro se litigants must follow the same rules of procedure that govern other litigants.").

[8] . FED. R. CIV. P. 8(a)(2). For further discussion on Rule 8 pleading requirements, see

CHARLES ALAN WRIGHT & MARY KAY KANE, LAW OF FEDERAL COURTS § 68 (6th ed. 2002).

[9]. The Rules arose out of an evolving American movement away from the formal rigidity of the common law pleading practice and toward a more simplified pleading system. *See* JACK FRIEDENTHAL ET AL., CIVIL PROCEDURE § 5.1 (4th ed. 2005); WRIGHT & KANE, §§ 66, 68. In accord with this movement, the Supreme Court promulgated the Rules in 1938. *See* FRIEDENTHAL ET AL., § 5.7, at 267. Of particular note, Rule 8 simplified and liberalized the federal pleading standard, creating a process in which the primary function of the complaint is to give fair notice to the adverse party. *See* FRIEDENTHAL ET AL., § 5.7; WRIGHT & KANE, § 68, at 471.

[10]. Swierkiewicz v. Sorema N. A., 534 U.S. 506, 514 (2002) ("The liberal notice pleading of Rule 8(a) is the starting point of a simplified pleading system, which was adopted to focus litigation on the merits of a claim.").

[11]*See* FRIEDENTHAL ET AL., , § 5.7; WRIGHT & KANE, , § 68, at 470-71, 473-74 (both noting that the Rules include techniques such as discovery and summary judgment to fill the roles of determining all the facts, narrowing the issues, and providing speedy disposition); *see also Swierkiewicz*, 534 U.S. at 511-12 (stating that Rule 8(a) requires that a Title VII plaintiff plead enough to provide notice of the claim, but need not allege a prima facie case); United States v. N. Trust Co., 372 F.3d 886, 888 (7th Cir. 2004) ("Even with respect to elements of the plaintiff's claim, complaints need not plead facts or legal theories."); Fontana v. Haskin, 262 F.3d 871, 877 (9th Cir. 2001) ("Specific legal theories need not be pleaded so long as sufficient factual averments show that the claimant may be entitled to some relief."); Simonton v. Runyon, 232 F.3d 33, 36-37 (2d Cir. 2000) ("'[G]enerally a complaint that gives full notice of the circumstances giving rise to the plaintiff's claim for relief need not also correctly plead the legal theory or theories and statutory basis supporting the claim.'" (quoting Marbury Mgmt., Inc. v. Kohn, 629 F.2d 705, 712 n.4 (2d Cir. 1980))); C&F Packing Co. v. IBP, Inc., 224 F.3d 1296, 1306

(Fed. Cir. 2000) ("A complaint need not specify the correct legal theory, or point to the right statute, to survive a motion to dismiss."); Peavy v. WFAA-TV, Inc., 221 F.3d 158, 167 (5th Cir. 2000) ("'The form of the complaint is not significant if it alleges facts upon which relief can be granted, even if it fails to categorize correctly the legal theory giving rise to the claim.'" (quoting Dussouy v. Gulf Coast Inv. Corp., 660 F.2d 594, 604 (5th Cir. Nov. 1981))); Williams v. Midwest Airlines, 321 F. Supp. 2d 993, 994 (E.D. Wis. 2004) ("It is not necessary for a plaintiff to identify in the complaint the legal theories on which he intends to proceed.").

[12] . The Supreme Court initially addressed the function of a pleading in *Conley*, 355 U.S. at 47-48. The Court faced a challenge to the sufficiency of a complaint against a union by AfricanAmerican railway workers who had alleged racial discrimination in violation of federal law. *Id.* at 42-43. In upholding the sufficiency of the complaint, the Court clarified that the plaintiffs need not set out specific or detailed facts to support a claim for relief. *Id.* at 47. Rule 8 simply required "'a short and plain statement of the claim' that [would] give the defendant fair notice of what the plaintiff's claim [was] and the grounds upon which it rest[ed]." *Id.* The Court made clear that the plaintiff was not obligated to "detail the facts on which he base[d] his claim." *Id.* In giving effect to these notice pleading requirements and the directive of Federal Rule of Civil Procedure 8(f), which requires construction of pleadings "to do substantial justice," the Supreme Court made clear that "[t]he Federal Rules reject the approach that pleading is a game of skill in which one misstep by counsel may be decisive to the outcome and accept the principle that the purpose of pleading is to facilitate a proper decision on the merits." *Id.* at 48; *accord* Richard L. Marcus, *The Revival of Fact Pleading Under the Federal Rules of Civil Procedure*, 86 COLUM. L. REV. 433, 434 (1986) (noting that "*Conley v. Gibson* put the Supreme Court on record as clearly favoring the liberal view [of pleading.

[13] 355 U.S. 41 (1957), *abrogated by* Bell Atl. Corp. v. Twombly, 127 S. Ct. 1955, 1968-69 (2007).

[14] *Twombly*, 127 S. Ct. at 1969 (quoting Dura Pharm., Inc. v. Broudo, 544 U.S. 336, 347 (2005)).

[15] *See* Associated Gen. Contractors of Cal., Inc. v. Cal. Council of Carpenters, 459 U.S. 519, 526 (1983) ("It is not . . . proper to assume that the Union can prove facts that it has not alleged or that the defendants have violated the antitrust laws in ways that have not been alleged."); *see also McGregor*, 856 F.2d at 43 (stating that "'when a plaintiff . . . supplies facts to support his claim, we do not think that *Conley* imposes a duty on the courts to conjure up unpleaded facts that might turn a frivolous claim into a substantial one . . . . [W]hen a complaint omits facts that, if they existed, would clearly dominate the case, it seems fair to assume that those facts do not exist'" (quoting *O'Brien*, 544 F.2d at 546 n.3 (citations omitted))).

[16] . *See* Bell Atl. Corp. v. Twombly, 127 S. Ct. 1955, 1969-74 (2007).

[17] Prisoner litigation is a relatively recent phenomenon. *See* Brian Ostrom et al., *Congress, Courts and Corrections: An Empirical Perspective on the Prison Litigation Reform Act*, 78 NOTRE DAME L. REV. 1525, 1529-32 (2003);Margo Schlanger, *Civil Rights Injunctions Over Time: A Case Study of Jail and Prison Court Orders*, 81 N.Y.U. L. REV. 550, 558-64 (2006) [hereinafter Schlanger, *Civil Rights Injunctions*]; *see also* Drew Swank, *In Defense of Rules and Roles: The Need to Curb Extreme Forms of Pro Se Assistance and Accommodation in Litigation*, 54 AM. U. L. REV. 1537, 1539-46 (2005) (discussing a general rise of pro se litigation).

[18] The Supreme Court observed, "[A] good many judges and commentators have balked at taking the literal terms of the *Conley* passage as a pleading standard." *Id.* at 1969. Joining these critics, the Court added:

To be fair to the *Conley* Court, the passage should be understood in light of the opinion's preceding summary of the complaint's concrete allegations, which the Court quite reasonably understood as amply stating a claim for relief. But the passage so often quoted fails to mention this understanding on the part of the Court, and after puzzling the profession for 50 years, this famous observation has earned its retirement. The phrase is best forgotten as an incomplete, negative gloss on an accepted pleading standard: once a claim has been stated adequately, it may be supported by showing any set of facts consistent with the allegations in the complaint.

[19]. Warth v. Seldin, 422 U.S. 490, 501 (1975) (recognizing the *Conley* pleading standard, but adding that "it is within the trial court's power to allow or to require the plaintiff to supply, by amendment to the complaint or by affidavits, further particularized allegations of fact deemed supportive of plaintiff's standing"); *see also* Papasan v. Allain, 478 U.S. 265, 286 (1986) (stating that on review of the sufficiency of a complaint, the court is "not bound to accept as true a legal conclusion couched as a factual allegation").

[20]. *Twombly*, 127 S. Ct. at 1959 (quoting FED. R. CIV. P. 8(a)(2)).

[21]. *See* O'Brien, 544 F.2d at 546 n.3 ("[W]hen a plaintiff under 42 U.S.C. § 1983 supplies facts to support his claim, we do not think that [*Conley*] imposes a duty on the courts to conjure up unpleaded facts that might turn a frivolous claim of unconstitutional official action into a substantial one."); *see also* Butz v. Economou, 438 U.S. 478, 507-08 (1978) (dictum) (suggesting that "[i]nsubstantial" cases can be dismissed despite "artful pleading"). *But cf.* Hazard, at 1672 ("Although Rule 8 permits a claimant to plead in vacuous terms, ordinarily plaintiffs in American litigation actually plead with the kind of specificity required elsewhere in the world."); Marcus, at 434 ("Although *Conley v. Gibson* put the Supreme Court on record as clearly favoring the liberal view, the actual application of its admonition in subsequent cases was more problematic.").

[22] *Car Carriers, Inc.*, 745 F.2d at 1106 (stating that "*Conley* has never been interpreted literally" (citing *Sutliff*, 727 F.2d at 654)).

[23]. *See* Ostrom et al., at 1529-32; Schlanger, *Civil Rights Injunctions*, at 558-61.

[24] *See, e.g.*, Cooper v. Pate, 378 U.S. 546, 546 (1964) (per curiam) (holding that a prisoner had stated a claim for relief under 42 U.S.C. § 1983 when he had alleged denial of "permission to purchase certain religious publications and denied other privileges enjoyed by other prisoners").

[25] Preiser v. Rodriguez, 411 U.S. 475, 498 (1973). The cases that the *Rodriguez* court acknowledged were *Haines v. Kerner*, 404 U.S. 1519 (1972); *Wilwording v. Swenson*, 404 U.S. 249 (1971); *Houghton v. Shafer*, 392 U.S. 639 (1968); and *Cooper*, 378 U.S. 546. The Court found that such cases "establish that a § 1983 action is a proper remedy for a state prisoner who is making a constitutional challenge to the conditions of his prison life, but not to the fact or length of his custody." *Rodriguez*, 411 U.S. at 499.

[26]. *See* Ostrom et al., at 1527-28; Edward Rubin & Malcolm Feeley, *Judicial Policy Making and Litigation Against the Government*, 5 U. PA. J. CONST. L. 617, 618-19 (2003) (discussing role of court in creating prison reform policy); Schlanger, *Civil Rights Injunctions*, *supra*, at 558-69; *see also* Gates v. Cook, 376 F.3d 323 (5th Cir. 2004) (class action brought by death row inmates housed in Unit 32-C at the Mississippi State Penitentiary, involving numerous allegations concerning unconstitutional living conditions on Death Row); Armstrong v. Davis, 275 F.3d 849 (9th Cir. 2001) (class action brought by disabled California prisoners who obtained system-wide injunctive relief for statutory violations); Harris v. Angelina County, 31 F.3d 331 (5th Cir. 1994) (affirming the district court injunction in a prisoner class action that imposed a cap on the number of prisoners as a remedy to unconstitutional conditions of confinement); Knop v. Johnson, 667 F. Supp. 467 (W.D. Mich. 1987) (class action prisoner suit in

which the district court ordered the prison to provide inmates with adequate winter clothing and adequate access to lavatory facilities).

[27] *See, e.g.*, Farmer v. Brennan, 511 U.S. 825, 832 (1994) (stating that prison officials' deliberate indifference to substantial risk of serious harm, including risk of harm from other prisoners, may violate the Eighth Amendment and is, therefore, actionable in a § 1983 proceeding); Estelle v. Gamble, 429 U.S. 97, 103-05 (1976) (stating that deliberate indifference to a prisoner's medical needs may violate the Eighth Amendment and, therefore, is actionable in a §1983 proceeding); *see also* Porter v. Nussle, 534 U.S. 516, 520 (2002) (involving an inmate's allegations of "a prolonged and sustained pattern of harassment and intimidation"); Lenz v. Wade 490 F.3d 991, 993-94 (8th Cir. 2007) (involving a prisoner's allegation of excessive force).

[28] . *See* Bell Atl. Corp. v. Twombly, 127 S. Ct. 1955, 1969-74 (2007).

[29] . The Supreme Court observed, "[A] good many judges and commentators have balked at taking the literal terms of the *Conley* passage as a pleading standard." *Id.* at 1969. Joining these critics, the Court added:

> To be fair to the *Conley* Court, the passage should be understood in light of the opinion's preceding summary of the complaint's concrete allegations, which the Court quite reasonably understood as amply stating a claim for relief. But the passage so often quoted fails to mention this understanding on the part of the Court, and after puzzling the profession for 50 years, this famous observation has earned its retirement. The phrase is best forgotten as an incomplete, negative gloss on an accepted pleading standard: once a claim has been stated adequately, it may be supported by showing any set of facts consistent with the allegations in the complaint.

[30] While prisoner litigation expanded dramatically, many pro se prisoner claims were dismissed as frivolous. *See* Jon Newman, *Pro Se Prisoner Litigation: Looking for Needles in Haystacks*, 62 BROOK. L. REV. 519, 519 (1996). By the mid-1990s, both types—class-action suits and suits raising individual prisoner claims—of prisoner litigation came under significant scrutiny and a great deal of criticism. *See, e.g.*, Lynn Branham, *The Prison Litigation Reform Act's Enigmatic Exhaustion Requirement: What It Means and What Congress, Courts and Correctional Officials Can Learn From It*, 86 CORNELL L. REV. 483, 520-26 (2001) (noting the mid-1990's responses of (1) state attorney generals, (2) Congress and (3) the Second Circuit); Newman, *supra*, at 520-26; Ostrom et al., *supra* note 24, at 1525-27; Kermit Roosevelt III, *Exhaustion under the Prison Litigation Reform Act: The Consequence of Procedural Error*, 52 EMORY L.J. 1771, 177173 (2003); Schlanger, *Civil Rights Injunctions*, *supra* note 24, at 589-602; Margo Schlanger, *Inmate Litigation*, 116 HARV. L. REV. 1555, 1626-33 (2003) [hereinafter Schlanger, *Inmate Litigation*]; Mark Tushnet & Larry Yackle, *Symbolic Statutes and Real Laws: The Pathologies of the Antiterrorism and Effective Death Penalty Act and the Prison Litigation Reform Act*, 47 DUKE L.J. 1, 18-20 (1997); *see generally* Michael Zachary, *Dismissal of Federal Actions and Appeals Under 28 U.S.C. §§1915(e)(2) and 1915a(b), 42 U.S.C. § 1997e(c) and The Inherent Authority of the Federal Courts: (A) Procedures for Screening and Dismissing Cases; (B) Special Problems Posed By the "Delusional" or "Wholly Incredible" Complaint*, 43 N.Y.L. SCH. L. REV. 975 (1999-2000) (discussing statutory changes PLRA brought to prisoner litigation).

[32] *See, e.g.*, Pomales v. Celulares Telefonica, Inc., 342 F.3d 44, 49 n.4 (1st Cir. 2003) ("[Plaintiff's] temporary pro se status did not absolve her of the need to comply with the Federal Rules of Civil Procedure or the district court's procedural rules."); Creative Gifts, Inc. v. UFO, 235 F.3d 540, 549 (10th Cir. 2000) ("Although pro se

litigants get the benefit of more generous treatment in some respects, they must nonetheless follow the same rules of procedure that govern other litigants."); LoSacco v. City of Middletown, 71 F.3d 88, 92 (2d Cir. 1995) ("Although [pro se] litigants should be afforded latitude, they 'generally are required to inform themselves regarding procedural rules and to comply with them.'" (quoting Edwards v. INS, 59 F.3d 5, 8 (2d Cir. 1995) (citation omitted)).

[33] *See, e.g.*, Pierce v. City of Miami, 176 F. App'x 12, 14 (11th Cir. 2006) (noting that "although pro se litigants are still bound by rules of procedure, . . . they should not be held to the same level of knowledge as an attorney"); *In re* T.R. Acquisition Corp., No. 99-5013, 1999 WL 753335, at *1 n.1 (2d Cir. Sept. 16, 1999) (noting that "[pro se] litigants . . . generally lack specific knowledge of . . . legal procedures").

[34] For example, Rule 56(c) requires a party to present evidence if the adversary's motion for summary judgment would otherwise reflect the absence of a genuine issue of material fact. FED. R. CIV. P. 56(c). Nonetheless, "[t]he majority of circuits have held that a pro se litigant is entitled to notice of the consequences of a summary judgment motion and the requirements of the summary judgment rule." United States v. Ninety-Three (93) Firearms, 2003 FED App. 0157P, at 20, 330 F.3d 414, 427 (6th Cir. 2003) (citing cases from the Second, Fourth, Seventh, Ninth, Tenth, Eleventh, and D.C. Circuits) (footnote omitted).

[35] *See, e.g.*, Nasious v. Two Unknown B.I.C.E. Agents, 492 F.3d 1158, 1162 (10th Cir. 2007) (noting that "a district court may, without abusing its discretion, enter [an order dismissing a pro se complaint for failure to comply with Rule 8] without attention to *any particular procedures*").

[36] . *See, e.g., id.* (noting that no particular warning must be given, but that a number of criteria should be considered before dismissing a pro se complaint).

[37] . *Id.* at 1163; *see also* Howard Eisenberg, *Rethinking Prisoner Civil Rights Cases and the Provision of Counsel*, 17 S. ILL. U. L.J. 417, 441-44 (1993) (discussing a prisoner's ability as a pro se plaintiff to draft viable complaints and the responses of the courts to liberally construe such pro se pleadings).

[38] . *Id.* at 1163; *see also* Howard Eisenberg, *Rethinking Prisoner Civil Rights Cases and the Provision of Counsel*, 17 S. ILL. U. L.J. 417, 441-44 (1993) (discussing a prisoner's ability as a pro se plaintiff to draft viable complaints and the responses of the courts to liberally construe such pro se pleadings).

[39] . *Nasious*, 492 F.3d at 1163 n.5 ("[W]e expect counsel to know the pleading rules of the road without being given personal notice of them by the district court. Our concern here is with the [pro se] litigant unschooled in the law.").

[40] . *See* Bell Atl. Corp. v. Twombly, 127 S. Ct. 1955, 1974 (2007)

[41] . *See, e.g.*, Eisenberg, *supra* note 36, at 443-44 (discussing courts' treatment of pro se prisoners); Marcus, at 477 (discussing the disproportionate treatment of pro se prisoners in court dismissals of their complaints).

[42] . *See* Schlanger, *Civil Rights Injunctions*, at 558-64 (discussing the prisoners' pro se litigation success in creating institutional change of the early 1960s and 1970s); Swank, at 1552-53 (discussing a court based pro se assistance program).

[43] Ostrom et al., at 1529-60 (noting the historical trends in treatment of pro se prisoner claims both before and after the enactment of the PLRA and the statistical analysis of case dismissals corresponding with those timelines); Schlanger, *Civil Rights Injunctions*, at 558-69; *see also* Swank, at 1548 (noting the negative anecdotal impressions of pro se litigants).

[44] *See, e.g.*, Smith v. N.Y. Presbyterian Hosp., 254 F. App'x 68, 70 (2d Cir. 2007); Harbulak v. Suffolk County, 654 F.2d 194, 198 (2d Cir. 1981).

⁴⁵When an attorney appears pro se, some courts have decided whether to liberally construe the pleadings based on whether the litigant was practicing law at the time. *Compare Harbulak*, 654 F.2d at 198 (holding that because a pro se litigant was a practicing lawyer, he was not entitled to "the special consideration customarily" available to unrepresented parties), *with N.Y. Presbyterian Hosp.*, 254 F. App'x at 70 (even though "licensed attorneys" need not be afforded special "pleading consideration" when they appear without legal representation, the plaintiff was entitled to treatment as a pro se litigant because she had "not practiced law for years" as a result of "psychiatric impairments"). When the party is not an attorney, some courts have still applied "a sliding scale of liberality" depending on the litigant's level of experience in the legal system. *E.g.*, Standley v. Dennison, No. 9:05-CV-1033 (GLS/GHL), 2007 WL 2406909, at *7-8 (N.D.N.Y. Aug. 21, 2007); Holsey v. Bass, 519 F. Supp. 395, 407 n.27 (D. Md. 1981); *see also* Michael J. Mueller, Note, *Abusive Pro Se Plaintiffs in the Federal Courts: Proposals for Judicial Control*, 18 U. MICH. J.L. REFORM 93, 98 n.14 (1984) ("Some courts have adopted a 'sliding scale of liberality' that places experienced pro se litigants somewhere between the uninitiated and trained lawyers.").

⁴⁶Many legal scholars have written about the political, social and judicial reaction to the prisoner litigation of the 1960s and 1970s. *See generally* Branham, at 484-97; Ostrom et al., at 1525-32; Schlanger, *Civil Rights Injunctions*, at 5506 12; Schlanger, *Inmate Litigation*, , at 1590-1627; Zachary, (comparing throughout prisoner litigation pre-PLRA and post-PLRA).

⁴⁷*See* Cynthia Gray, *Reaching Out or Overreaching: Judicial Ethics and Self-Represented Litigants*, 27 J. NAT'L ASSOC. ADMIN. L. JUDICIARY 97, 101 (2007) ("Case after case announces 'the hoary but still vigorous rule' that self-represented litigants are held to the same standard as attorneys - and then case after case, often the same cases, describes exceptions to that rule and the special treatment trial judges should accord to those without attorneys."

(quoting Gamet v. Blanchard, 111 Cal. Rptr. 2d 439, 447 (Dist. Ct. App. 2001))).

[48] It is important to remember that the *Conley* standard preceded the *Twombly* standard.

[49] *Haines*, 404 U.S. at 520-21; *see also* Estelle v. Gamble, 429 U.S. 97, 112 (1976) (Stevens, J., dissenting) (stating that the test in *Haines* is "whether the Court can say with assurance on the basis of the complaint that, beyond any doubt, no set of facts could be proved that would entitle the plaintiff to relief").

[50] *See* Erickson v. Pardus, 127 S. Ct. 2197, 2200 (2007) (per curiam) (in a post-*Twombly* decision involving pro se prisoners, the Court noted that pro se pleadings must "'be liberally construed'" and are "'held to less stringent standards than formal pleadings drafted by lawyers'"

[51] *Haines*, 404 U.S. at 520-21 (quoting Conley v. Gibson, 355 U.S. 41, 45-46 (1957)).

[52] One student commentator notes:

> [The] limitation [in *Haines*] is read differently by each court in terms of how liberally, and to which pleadings the rule applies. This results in inconsistent treatment of pro se litigants in the lower courts. For example, some courts rely upon the Supreme Court's rationale in *Haines* to fashion a relaxed set of pro se standards for procedural conformity, particularly when dealing with summary judgment proceedings, compliance with discovery rules, the imposition of sanctions, and the introduction of evidence. A greater number of courts ... take a more traditional approach and extend this sort of pleading leniency only to the substantive issues raised, while continuing to strictly enforce compliance with procedural requirements by pro se litigants.
>
> Tiffany Buxton, Note, *Foreign Solutions to the U.S. Pro Se Phenomenon*, 34 CASE W. RES. J. INT'L L. 103, 117-18 (2002) (footnotes omitted).

[53] Kane v. Winn, 319 F. Supp. 2d 162, 175 (D. Mass. 2004).

[54] Eisenberg, at 443 (footnote omitted) (citing and quoting Douglas A. Blaze, *Presumed Frivolous: Application of Stringent Pleading Requirements in Civil Rights Litigation*, 31 WM. & MARY L. REV. 935, 971-72 (1990)).

[55] *See, e.g.*, McDonald v. Hall, 610 F.2d 16, 20 (1st Cir. 1979) (Campbell, J., dissenting) (suggesting that the majority "ben[t] over backwards to excuse the omission of allegations of the basic facts needed to make out a possible claim").

[56] Prison Litigation Reform Act of 1995, Pub. L. No. 104-134, § 101, 110 Stat. 1321 (1996).

[57] Antiterrorism and Effective Death Penalty Act of 1996, Pub. L. No. 104-32, 110 Stat. 1214 (1996).

[58] . Prison Litigation Reform Act of 1995, 42 U.S.C. § 1997e(a) (2000).

[59] . Prison Litigation Reform Act of 1995, 28 U.S.C. § 1915(g) (2000).

[60] . 42 U.S.C. § 1997e(a) (2000).

[61] . 404 U.S. 519 (1972) (per curiam).

[62] . As noted earlier, often prisoner complaints involve inartful, mislabeled or muddled allegations and claims for relief. Often the litigants are poorly educated and are unable to craft a document like a lawyer. These defects often mean that the court has to wade through the pleading to discern what the allegations are, what claims for relief these allegations support, and sometimes even who the alleged defendants are. *See, e.g.*, Crooks v. Nix, 872 F.2d 800, 801 (8th Cir. 1989) (employing liberal construction of pleading to discern relevant defendants and claims); Haley v. Dormire, 845 F.2d 1488, 1490 (8th Cir. 1988) (reversing dismissal of pro se prisoner complaint because when "read expansively" the complaints set forth sufficient claims for relief); Massop v. Coughlin, 770 F.2d 299, 301 (2d Cir. 1985) (per curiam) (although district court could not find a constitutional claim based on the

allegations in the prisoner's complaint, Second Circuit remanded finding that applying liberal standard of review, prisoner set forth sufficient allegations that the prison guard intentionally injured him); Marshall v. Brierley, 461 F.2d 929, 930 (3rd Cir. 1972) (reviewing complaint filed by a prisoner with "only minimal literary skills" and finding sufficient grounds to allow complaint to go forward).

[63] . Judge Easterbrook explained, "A drafter who lacks a legal theory is likely to bungle the complaint (and the trial); you need a theory to decide which facts to allege and prove. But the complaint need not identify a legal theory, and specifying an incorrect theory is not fatal." Bartholet v. Reishauer A.G. (Zurich), 953 F.2d 1073, 1078 (7th Cir. 1992).

[64] Professors Wright and Miller state:

> The federal rules, and the decisions construing them, evince a belief that when a party has a valid claim, he should recover on it regardless of his counsel's failure to perceive the true basis of the claim at the pleading stage, provided always that a late shift in the thrust of the case will not prejudice the other party in maintaining a defense upon the merits.

[65] CHARLES ALAN WRIGHT & ARTHUR MILLER, FEDERAL PRACTICE AND PROCEDURE: CIVIL § 1219, at 281-83 (3d ed. 2004) (footnote omitted).

[66] . In many cases, courts dismiss prisoner pleadings based on the failure of the prisoner to set out or adequately explain his claims and the court does not engage in an effort to create claims of relief for the plaintiff or to try to help the plaintiff in setting out his claims. *See, e.g.*, Richards v. Johnson, 115 F. App'x 677 (5th Cir. 2004) (dismissing complaint where there was lack of specificity in claims and defendants); McDonald v. Hall, 610 F.2d 16 (1st Cir. 1979) (stating "[o]ur duty to be 'less stringent' with pro se complaints does not require us to conjure up unpled allegations").

⁶⁷ . In other cases, the courts appear to be more liberal in finding claims that may go forward in a § 1983 action. *See, e.g.*, Dillier v. Williams, No. 93-56380, 1994 WL 10005, at *1-2 (9th Cir. Jan. 13, 1994) (applying liberal pleading standard to inartful complaint, court found district court erred in dismissal of complaint); Roundtree v. N.Y. Dep't of Corr., No. CV-94-3833 (CPS), 1995 WL 428654, at *5 (E.D.N.Y. July 1,1995) (noting that although inartfully pled, the plaintiff nonetheless stated a claim with respect to constitutional deprivation due to prison transfer decision); *see also* Marshall v. Brierley, 461 F.2d 929, 930 (3rd Cir. 1972) (reviewing complaint filed by a prisoner with "only minimal literary skills" and finding sufficient grounds to allow complaint to go forward).

⁶⁸ . *See, e.g.*, Burgos v. Hopkins, 14 F.3d 787, 790 (2d Cir. 1994) ("Because Burgos is a pro se litigant, we read his supporting papers liberally, and will interpret them to raise the strongest arguments that they suggest."); White v. Wyrick, 530 F.2d 818, 819 (8th Cir. 1976) (per curiam) ("[W]e note that petitioner appears pro se and is entitled to have his pleadings interpreted liberally and his petition should be construed to encompass any allegation stating federal relief . . . .").

⁶⁹The exhaustion requirement can be found at 42 U.S.C. § 1997e(a) (2000).

⁷⁰*See, e.g.*, Patel v. Fleming, 415 F.3d 1105, 1109-11 (10th Cir. 2005) (dismissing prisoner's pro se complaint for failure to timely submit a written administrative remedy request even though plaintiff claimed he was late in submitting because of an attempt to intentionally resolve his second hand smoke damages); Bey v. Johnson, 2005 FED App. 0194P, 407 F.3d 801, 805-07 (6th Cir. 2005) (adopting the "total exhaustion rule" so that any and all available remedies must have been exhausted before a prisoner could bring any claims that were even remotely connected to potential administrative remedies), *vacated and remanded by* 127 S. Ct. 1212 (2007); Graves v. Norris, 218 F.3d 884, 885-86 (8th

Cir. 2000) (per curiam) (dismissing the claim because "it is clear from the record that at least some of plaintiffs claims were unexhausted"). The Supreme Court ultimately rejected this approach. Jones v. Bock, 549 U.S. 199, 219 (2007) (concluding that "exhaustion is not *per se* inadequate . . . . [L]eav[ing] it to the court below in the first instance to determine the sufficiency of the exhaustion in these cases").

[71] *E.g.*, Ortiz v. McBride, 380 F.3d 649, 651 (2d Cir. 2004) (observing Second Circuit conclusion that complete dismissal is not required under § 1997e).

[72] Prison Litigation Reform Act of 1995, 28 U.S.C. § 1915(g) (2000).

[73] *See, e.g.*, Dubuc v. Johnson, 314 F.3d 1205, 1209 (10th Cir. 2003) (discussing "the irony that ascertaining whether a particular prisoner litigant has accumulated at least three strikes may require the use of more judicial resources than addressing the prisoner's claims on the merits").

[74] *See* Pointer v. Wilkinson, 2007 FED App. 0363P, at 7, 502 F.3d 369, 377 (6th Cir. 2007) ("[W]e hold that where a complaint is dismissed in part without prejudice for failure to exhaust administrative remedies and in part with prejudice because 'it is frivolous, malicious, or fails to state a claim upon which relief may be granted,' the dismissal should be counted as a strike under 28 U.S.C. § 1915(g)."); Comeaux v. Cockrell, 72 F. App'x 54, 55 (5th Cir. 2003) (per curiam) ("The district court could dismiss part of [the plaintiff's] complaint as malicious, which counted as a strike under 28 U.S.C. § 1915(g), even though the case was ultimately dismissed for failure to comply with court orders."); Faust v. Parke, No. 96-3881, 1997 WL 284598, at *3 (7th Cir. May 22, 1997) (stating that a dismissal "counts as a strike" under § 1915(g), notwithstanding the court's decision not to retain jurisdiction over a constructive fraud claim); Eady v. Lappin, No. 9:05-CV0824, 2007 WL 1531879, at *2 (N.D.N.Y. May 22, 2007) (adopting magistrate judge's finding that "a plaintiff might earn a

strike because some of his claims were dismissed for frivolousness, maliciousness or failure to state a claim"); Shaw v. Weaks, No. 06-2024-B/V, 2006 WL 1049307, at *6 n.13 (W.D. Tenn. Apr. 20, 2006) ("The fact that some of plaintiff's claims in this action have been dismissed for failure to exhaust does not preclude the imposition of a strike on the basis of claims that were dismissed for failure to state a claim or as frivolous."); Luedtke v. Bertrand, 32 F. Supp. 2d 1074, 1076 n.1 (E.D. Wis. 1999) (holding that dismissal of a corresponding state law claim, without prejudice, based on a lack of federal subject-matter jurisdiction, "does not, and should not, disqualify the case from being counted as a 'strike' for purposes of § 1915(g)").

[75] *See* Prison Litigation Reform Act of 1995, 28 U.S.C. § 1915(g) (2000).

[76] *See, e.g.*, United States v. Castro, 540 U.S. 375 (2003).

[77] *See* Jon O. Newman, *Rethinking Fairness: Perspectives on the Litigation Process*, 94 YALE L.J. 1643, 1646 (1985) [hereinafter Newman, *Rethinking Fairness*] ("Fairness is the fundamental concept that guides our thinking [as Judges] about substantive and procedural law.").

[78] *See, e.g.*, Lois Bloom & Helen Hershkoff, *Federal Courts, Magistrate Judges, and the Pro Se Plaintiff*, 16 NOTRE DAME J.L. ETHICS & PUB. POL'Y 475, 515 (2002) ("[C]ourts and commentators are thus coming to recognize the authority, if not the responsibility, of a judge to depart from the ethical norms of adversarial justice in order to ensure a fair and accurate result and, in particular, to take an activist stance in cases involving unrepresented litigants."); Newman, *Rethinking Fairness*, at 1649 ("[A]lthough we scrupulously strive to achieve a fair outcome in the individual dispute, we rarely consider how to be fair to all who use or would like to use the litigation system.").

[79] The Ninth Circuit Court of Appeals urged equal treatment for pro se litigants in ordinary civil cases, stating, "Trial courts generally do not intervene to save litigants from their choice of counsel, even

when the lawyer loses the case because he fails to file opposing papers. A litigant who chooses *himself* as legal representative should be treated no differently." Jacobsen v. Filler, 790 F.2d 1362, 1364-65 (9th Cir. 1986) (footnote omitted).

[80]. *See* Michael L. Moffitt, *Customized Litigation: The Case for Making Civil Procedure Negotiable*, 75 GEO. WASH. L. REV. 461, 521 (2007) ("[T]he reality on the ground is that, even today, no two trials look exactly alike, not only because the particular facts of the dispute are different, but also because some degree of customization already happens.").

[81]. Newman, *Rethinking Fairness*, at 1648.

[82]. *See* Pruitt v. Mote, 503 F.3d 647, 664 (7th Cir. 2007) ("[A] judge is constrained by a duty of impartiality, and whatever he might do to help an unrepresented litigant, he cannot be that individual's advocate."); *see also* MODEL CODE OF JUDICIAL CONDUCT Canon 2 (2007) ("A judge shall perform the duties of judicial office impartially, competently, and dligently.").

[83]. Judges are prohibited from practicing law. MODEL CODE OF JUDICIAL CONDUCTR. 3.10 (2007) ("A judge shall not practice law."); CODE OF CONDUCT FOR UNITED STATES JUDGES Canon 5(F) ("A judge should not practice law."). Giving legal advice is a basic characteristic of legal practice, as the Supreme Court noted: "Explaining the details of federal habeas procedure and calculating statutes of limitations are tasks normally and properly performed by trained counsel as a matter of course. Requiring district courts to advise a [pro se] litigant in such a manner would undermine district judges' role as impartial decisionmakers." Pliler v. Ford, 542 U.S. 225, 231 (2004); *see also In re* Reynoso, 477 F.3d 1117, 1125 (9th Cir. 2007) (remarking that under state law, the practice of law generally includes "legal advice"). Thus, a judge cannot ethically give legal advice to any of the parties, regardless of whether they are pro se.

[84] *See* Massachusetts v. EPA, 549 U.S. 497, 516 (2007) ("It is . . . familiar learning that no justiciable 'controversy' exists when parties . . . ask for an advisory opinion . . . .") (citation omitted); *see also* Asahi Glass Co. v. Pentech Pharms., Inc., 289 F. Supp. 2d 986, 989-90 (N.D. Ill. 2003) (noting that federal courts cannot issue advisory opinions and that "judges are not authorized to issue legal advice").

[85] . One commentator explains:

> Justice is blind and employs scales to ensure procedural fairness, an ideal fundamental to the Constitution's due process tradition. Procedure constrains judicial sight and provides criteria of relevance for what kinds of things Justitia might properly see. Like the mechanics of paired scales, procedure provides the mechanics for fair outcomes through the blind weighing of competing claims.

Thomas P. Crocker, *Envisioning the Constitution*, 57 AM. U. L. REV. 1, 27 (2007).

[86] . For example, in 2007, the American Bar Association approved a comment to accompany the *Model Code of Judicial Conduct*, which would allow judges "to make reasonable accommodations to ensure pro se litigants the opportunity to have their matters fairly heard." MODEL CODE OF JUDICIAL CONDUCT R. 2.2 cmt. 4 (2007). The *Reporter's Explanation of Changes* noted that the comment was designed to "level[] the playing field" by ensuring a "fair hearing" but not "an unfair advantage" for pro se litigants. MODEL CODE OF JUDICIAL CONDUCT R. 2.2, reporter's explanation of changes cmt. 4 (2007), *available at*www.abanet.org/judicialethics/mcjc2007.pdf. 1988 ("The rules primarily prohibit . . . court players from giving legal advice to unrepresented litigants.").

[87] . *See* Laber v. Harvey, 438 F.3d 404, 413 n.3 (4th Cir. 2006) ("In interpreting a pro se complaint, . . . our task is not to discern the

unexpressed intent of the plaintiff, but what the words in the complaint mean.").

[88]. Haines v. Kerner, 404 U.S. 519, 520 (1972) (per curiam) (noting that pro se complaints are held to "less stringent standards than formal pleadings drafted by lawyers").

[89]. So named because the hearings were established in *Spears v. McCotter*, 766 F.2d 179 (5th Cir. 1985), *abrogated by Nietzke v. Williams*, 490 U.S. 319 (1989).

[90]. An example of the procedure is reflected in *Davis v. Scott*, 157 F.3d 1003 (5th Cir. 1998). There the appeals court held that the magistrate judge had acted within his discretion in developing and ultimately dismissing a prisoner's Eighth Amendment claims. *Id.* at 1005. The Fifth Circuit Court of Appeals went on to explain:

This is quite a different thing from saying that the magistrate judge has a duty to interrogate the pro se plaintiff in such a way as to exhaust conceivable causes of action. The magistrate judge has no such duty. Instead, the *Spears* procedure affords the plaintiff an opportunity to verbalize his complaints, in a manner of communication more comfortable to many prisoners. But the plaintiff remains the master of his complaint and is, in the end, the person responsible for articulating the facts that give rise to a cognizable claim. *Id.* at 1005-06.

[91]. Will v. Mich. Dept. of State Police, 491 U.S. 58, 71, 109 S. Ct. 2304, 105 L. Ed. 2d 45 (1989).

[92] Quern v. Jordan, 440 U.S. 332, 340-45, 99 S. Ct. 1139, 59 L. Ed. 2d 358 (1979); see Lawson v. Shelby Cnty., Tenn., 211 F.3d 331, 335 (6th Cir. 2000) ("[T]he [Eleventh] Amendment prohibits suits against a 'state' in federal court whether for injunctive, declaratory or monetary relief.").

[93] S & M Brands, Inc. v. Cooper, 527 F.3d 500, 507 (6th Cir. 2008). See Berndt v. Tennessee, 796 F.2d 879, 881 (6th Cir. 1986) (noting

that Tennessee has not waived immunity to suits under § 1983); Hafer v. Melo, 502 U.S. 21, 25, 112 S. Ct. 358, 116 L. Ed. 2d 301 (1991) (reaffirming that Congress did not abrogate states' immunity when it passed § 1983).

[94] Hodgers-Durgin v. De La Vina, 199 F.3d 1037, 1042 (9th Cir. 1999) (quoting O'Shea v. Littleton, 414 U.S. 488, 502, 94 S. Ct. 669, 38 L. Ed. 2d 674 (1974)).

[95] MAI Sys. Corp. v. Peak Computer, Inc., 991 F.2d 511, 516-517 (9th Cir. 1993) (quoting Diamontiney v. Borg, 918 F.2d 793, 795 (9th Cir. 1990)).

[96] **AGCC v. Coalition for Economic Equity, 950 F.2d 1401, 1410 (9th Cir. 1991).**

[97] Diamontiney v. Borg, 918 F.2d 793, 796 (9th Cir. 1990).

[98] Devose v. Herrington, 42 F.3d 470, 471 (8th Cir. 1994) (Eighth Amendment claim cannot provide basis for preliminary injunction against alleged acts in retaliation for filing claim).

[99] **Kaimowitz v. Orlando, Fla., 122 F.3d 41, 43 (11th Cir. 1997).**

[100] Tsao v. Desert Palace, Inc., 698 F.3d 1128, 1138-39 (9th Cir. 2012); Buckner v. Toro, 116 F.3d 450, 452 (11th Cir. 1997).

[101] Barren v. Harrington, 152 F.3d 1193, 1194 (9th Cir. 1998).

[102] Cortez v. County of Los Angeles, 294 F.3d 1186, 1188 (9th Cir. 2001).

[103] Monell v. Dep't of Soc. Servs., 436 U.S. 658, 691, 98 S. Ct. 2018, 56 L. Ed. 2d 611 (1978); Taylor v. List, 880 F.2d 1040, 1045 (9th Cir. 1989).

[104] Canell v. Lightner, 143 F.3d 1210, 1213 (9th Cir. 1998).

[105] **Clement v. Gomez, 298 F.3d 898, 905 (9th Cir. 2002) (a plaintiff must allege facts to support that "in light of the duties assigned to specific officers or employees, the need for more or different training is [so] obvious, and the inadequacy so likely to result in violations of constitutional rights, that the**

policy[]makers . . . can reasonably be said to have been deliberately indifferent to the need." (quoting City of Canton v. Harris, 489 U.S. 378, 390, 109 S. Ct. 1197, 103 L. Ed. 2d 412 (1989)))."

[106] *Monell v. New York City Dep't of Soc. Servs.*, 436 U.S. 658, 691, 98 S. Ct. 2018, 56 L. Ed. 2d 611(1978); *Everson v. Leis*, 556 F.3d 484, 495 (6th Cir. 2009).

[107] *Grinter v. Knight*, 532 F.3d 567, 575-76 (6th Cir. 2008); *Greene v. Barber*, 310 F.3d 889, 899 (6th Cir. 2002).

[108] *Summers v. Leis*, 368 F.3d 881, 888 (6th Cir. 2004).

[109] *Shehee v. Luttrell*, 199 F.3d 295, 300 (6th Cir. 1999).

[110] *Diamond v. Charles*, 476 U.S. 54, 64, 106 S. Ct. 1697, 90 L. Ed. 2d 48 (1986).

[111] **Smallwood v. McDonald, 805 F.2d 1036 (6th Cir. 1986).**

[112] *Walker v. Mich. Dep't of Corr.*, 128 F. App'x 441, 445 (6th Cir. 2005); *Argue v. Hofmeyer*, 80 F. App'x 427, 430 (6th Cir. 2003).

[113] *Knop v. Johnson*, 977 F.2d 996, 1014 (6th Cir. 1992); *Bellamy v. Bradley*, 729 F.2d 416, 421 (6th Cir. 1984).

[114] *Estelle v. Gamble*, 429 U.S. 97, 103-04, 97 S. Ct. 285, 50 L. Ed. 2d 251 (1976).

[115] **Comstock v. McCrary, 273 F.3d 693, 702 (6th Cir. 2001).**

[116] *Tsao v. Desert Palace, Inc.*, 698 F.3d 1128, 1138-39 (9th Cir. 2012); *Buckner v. Toro*, 116 F.3d 450, 452 (11th Cir. 1997).

[117] *George v. Sonoma Cnty. Sheriff's Dep't,* **732 F. Supp. 2d 922 (N.D.Cal. 2010) (inmate's survivors filed a § 1983 action for inadequate medical care, and court found that a private corporation could not be held liable for plaintiffs' injuries because they could not show that the violations occurred as a result of a policy, decision, or custom promulgated or endorsed by the private entity).**

[118] *Mabe v. San Bernardino Cnty., Dep't of Pub. Soc. Servs.*, 237 F.3d 1101, 1110-11 (9th Cir. 2001).

[119] L.A. Cnty., Cal. v. Humphries, 562 U.S. 29, 131 S. Ct. 447, 450-51, 178 L. Ed. 2d 460 (2010).

[120] *Jett v. Penner*, 439 F.3d 1091, 1096 (9th Cir. 2006) (citing *Estelle v. Gamble*, 429 U.S. 97, 104, 97 S. Ct. 285, 50 L. Ed. 2d 251 (1976)).

[121] *McGuckin v. Smith*, 974 F.2d 1050, 1059-60 (9th Cir. 1992), overruled on other grounds, *WMX Techs., Inc. v. Miller*, 104 F.3d 1133, 1136 (9th Cir. 1997) (en banc) (internal citation omitted).

[122] *Hallett v. Morgan*, 296 F.3d 732, 744 (9th Cir.2002) (internal citations and quotation marks omitted),

[123] *Wilhelm v. Rotman*, 680 F.3d 1113, 1122 (9th Cir. 2012) (citations omitted).

[124] Jackson v. McIntosh, 90 F.3d 330, 332 (9th Cir. 1996).

[125] *Hunt v. Dental Dep't*, 865 F.2d 198, 200 (9th Cir. 1989) (delay in providing medical treatment does not constitute *Eighth Amendment* violation unless delay was harmful).

[126] Conn. v. Mass., 282 U.S. 660, 674, 51 S. Ct. 286, 75 L. Ed. 602 (1931) (an injunction is only appropriate "to prevent existing or presently threatened injuries"); see Caribbean Marine Servs. Co. v. Baldrige, 844 F.2d 668, 674 (9th Cir. 1988).

[127] *See Snow v. McDaniel*, 681 F.3d 978, 988 (9th Cir. 2012) (where the treating physician and specialist recommended surgery, a reasonable jury could conclude that it was medically unacceptable for the non-treating, non-specialist physicians to deny recommendations for surgery), overruled in part on other grounds, *Peralta v. Dillard*, 744 F.3d 1076, 1082-83 (9th Cir. 2014); *Jones v. Simek*, 193 F.3d 485, 490 (7th Cir. 1999) (the defendant physician's refusal to follow the advice of treating specialists could constitute deliberate indifference to serious medical needs).

[128] *Ortiz v. City of Imperial, 884 F.2d 1312, 1314 (9th Cir. 1989)* ("access to medical staff is meaningless unless that staff is competent and can render competent care"); *see Estelle, 429 U.S. at 105* & n. 10 (the treatment received by a prisoner can be so bad that the treatment itself manifests deliberate indifference); *Lopez v. Smith, 203 F.3d 1122, 1132 (9th Cir. 2000)* (prisoner does not have to prove that he was completely denied medical care).

[129] *Jett v. Penner, 439 F.3d 1091, 1096 (9th Cir. 2006)* (quoting *Estelle v. Gamble, 429 U.S. 97, 104, 97 S. Ct. 285, 50 L. Ed. 2d 251 (1976)*).

[130] *Toguchi v. Chung, 391 F.3d 1051, 1060 (9th Cir. 2004).*

[131] *Farmer v. Brennan, 511 U.S. 825, 837, 114 S. Ct. 1970, 128 L. Ed. 2d 811 (1994).*

[132] Managing Editor, Boston College Journal of Law & Social Justice (2012–2103). Kyle T. Sullivan, *To Free or Not to Free: Rethinking Release Orders under the Prison Litigation Reform Act after Brown v. Plata*, 33 B.C.J.L. & Soc. Just. 419 (2013), http://lawdigitalcommons.bc.edu/jlsj/ vol33/iss2/6

[133] *See* Branham, at 537–39; Burtka, at 27–29; Amend, at 161–69.

[134] *See* Branham, at 537–39; Amend, at 168–69.

[135] *See Plata*, 131 S. Ct. at 1954 (Scalia, J., dissenting);Branham, at 537–39; Amend, at 162–65, 167–69.

[136] *See* Branham, at 537–39.

[137] *See Hearing on H.R. 4109*, at 4;Branham, at 537–39.

[138] *See Hearing on H.R. 4109*, at 4; Branham,at 537–38.

[139] *See* Branham,at 537–39.

[140] *See id.* at 488–89, 537–39.

[141] *See* U.S. Const. art. I, § 7, cl. 2–3. *See generally* INS v. Chadha, 462 U.S. 919 (1983) (holding that bills must be considered and approved by both houses of Congress and by the President in

order to become law); Branham, at 537–38. The Presentment Clause states in relevant part: "Every Bill which shall have passed the House of Representatives and the Senate, shall, before it become a Law, be presented to the President of the United States . . . ." U.S. Const. art. I, § 7, cl. 2.

[142]*See* U.S. Const. art. I, § 7, cl. 2–3; Branham, at 537–38.

[143]*See* Clinton v. New York, 524 U.S. 417, 421 (1998) (holding that allowing the President to strike individual provisions from appropriations bill and sign the modified bill into law violates the Presentment Clause of the Constitution);Branham, at 537–39.

[144]*See* U.S. Const. art. I, § 7, cl. 2; *Clinton*, 524 U.S. at 421; Branham, at 537–38.

[145]*See* U.S. Const. art. I, § 7, cl. 2–3; Branham, at 538; Amend, at 168–69.

[146]*See* U.S. Const. amend. VIII; Amend, at 161 (internal citation omitted).

[147]*See* Amend, 168.

[148]116 *See id.* at 488–89, 537–39.

[149]*See* U.S. Const. amends. V, XIV; Burtka, , at 27–28.

[150]*See* U.S. Const. amends. V, XIV; Burtka, at 27–28. Not every provision in the Bill of Rights is absolute; for example, it is settled law that, despite its absolute language, the First Amendment freedom of speech is qualified by the need to maintain order in society. *See* Erwin Chemerinsky, Constitutional Law 924–25 (3d ed. 2006).

[151]*See* Burtka, at 27–28; *see also*Hearing on H.R. 4109, at 1–2.

[152]*See* U.S. Const. art. V; Burtka, , at 27–28.

[153]*See* Plata v. Schwarzenegger, No. C01-1351 TEH, 2005 U.S. Dist. LEXIS 43796, at *1, *72–74 (N.D. Cal. Oct. 3, 2005) (outlining conclusions of law in the May 10, 2005, hearing on the Order to Show Cause), *aff'd*, Coleman v. Schwarzenegger, No. CIV S-90-0520 LKK JFM P, at 1, 6–9 (E.D. Cal. Aug. 4, 2009), *available at* http://www.ca9.uscourts.gov/datastore/general/

2009/08/04/Opinion%20&%20Order%20FINAL.pdf; Amend, at 162–63.

[154] Amend, at 164.

[155] *See* Prison Litigation Reform Act, 18 U.S.C. § 3626(a)(2)–(3) (2006); Amend, at 162, 164–65 (quoting *Plata*,2005 U.S. Dist. LEXIS 43796, at *72). 132 *See* § 3626(b); Amend, at 165–67.

[156] *See* Amend, at 162–167.

[157] *SeePlata*, 131 S. Ct. at 1953–54 (Scalia, J., dissenting); Branham, at 535.

[158] *See Plata*,131 S. Ct. at 1937–40; *id.* at 1951–53 (Scalia, J., dissenting); *id.* at 1959–60 (Alito, J., dissenting).

[159] *See id.* at 1951–53 (Scalia, J., dissenting).

[160] *See id.* at 1963–64 (Alito, J., dissenting).

[161] *See* Prison Litigation Reform Act, 18 U.S.C. § 3626(a)(1)(A) (2006).

[162] *See Plata*,131 S. Ct. at 1941–43; *id.* at 1950–51 (Scalia, J., dissenting); *id.* at 1965–67 (Alito, J., dissenting).

[163] *See id.* at 1953–54 (Scalia, J., dissenting); Branham,at 535.

[164] *42 U.S.C. § 1997e(a); Jones v. Bock, 549 U.S. 199, 202, 127 S. Ct. 910, 166 L. Ed. 2d 798 (2007); Jones v. Norris, 310 F.3d 610, 612 (8th Cir. 2002).*

[165] *Woodford v. Ngo, 548 U.S. 81, 92, 126 S. Ct. 2378, 165 L. Ed. 2d 368 (2006).*

[166] *Porter v. Nussle, 534 U.S. 516, 523, 122 S. Ct. 983, 152 L. Ed. 2d 12 (2002).*

[167] *Booth v. Churner, 532 U.S. 731, 741, 121 S. Ct. 1819, 149 L. Ed. 2d 958 (2001).*

[168] *Albino v. Baca, 747 F.3d 1162, 1169, 1172 (9th Cir. 2014).*

[169] Brown v. Valoff, 422 F.3d 926, 936 (9th Cir. 2005).

[170] **Wyatt v. Terhune, 315 F.3d 1108, 1120 (9th Cir. 2003), overruled in part on other grounds by Albino, 747 F.3d 1162.**

[171] *Reed-Bey v. Pramstaller, 603 F. 3d 322, 324 (6th Cir. 2010)* (citation omitted).

[172] *Curry v. Scott, 249 F.3d 493, 505 (6th Cir. 2001).*

[173] ACLU in its press release states

[174] **Arizona Department of Corrections September 21, 2012 to Karen Mullenix Wexford Health Sources**

[175] **Arizona Department of Corrections September 21, 2012 to Karen Mullenix Wexford Health Sources**

[176] Allegheny County ends its contract with Corizon Health Pittsburgh Post-Gazette by Molly Born

[177] Audit of Allegheny County Jail health provider says money being wasted BY AARON AUPPERLEE

[178] New Health Care Provider Picked for Oregon Jail after Audit Criticizes Corizon by Mark Wilson- Prison Legal News

[179] More Jurisdictions Don't Renew Corizon Contracts – Including Big Loss in New York City by Greg Dober - Prison Legal NewsOctober, 2015

[180] Civil lawsuit against Corizon Health Provider - By David Klugh, Anchor CHATHAM CO., GA (WTOC)

[181] Corizon Abandons Kentucky Jail Contract in Wake of Death and Lawsuits by David Reutter courier-journal.com

[182] 8.3 MILLION FOR JAIL DEATH -- LARGEST WRONGFUL DEATH CIVIL RIGHTS SETTLEMENT IN CALIFORNIA STATE HISTORY - Haddad & Sherwin.webloc

[183] **Fields v. Corizon Health, 490 Fed.Appx. 174 (11th Cir. 2012).**

[184] **SHIRLEY JENKINS, as Personal Representative for the Estate of Jovon Frazier, deceased, Plaintiff, v. CORIZON HEALTH,**

INC., Defendant. United States District Court, M.D. Florida, Tampa Division. Case No. 8:13-cv-2796-T-30TGW. May 20, 2016.

[185] DECLARATION OF TODD R. WILCOX in Parsons v Ryan

[186] EARL FARMER, Plaintiff, v. C.L. "BUTCH" OTTER; RANDY BLADES; MS. WAMBLE-FISHER; CATHY STEFFEN; CORIZON MEDICAL SERVICES; **IDAHO STATE DEPARTMENT OF** CORRECTION; and IDAHO STATE BOARD OF CORRECTION, Defendants. Case No. 1:14-cv-00345-BLW UNITED STATES DISTRICT COURT FOR THE DISTRICT OF IDAHO

[187] *Brown v. Valoff, 422 F.3d 926, 936 (9th Cir. 2005).*

[188] *Wyatt v. Terhune, 315 F.3d 1108, 1120 (9th Cir. 2003), overruled in part on other grounds by Albino, 747 F.3d 1162.*

[189] *See* 42 U.S.C. ~1997e(a); *see also Hall v. Reinke*, No. 1:13-cv-118-REB, 2014 U.S. Dist. LEXIS 136372, 2014 WL 4793955, at *6 (D. Idaho Sept. 25, 2014) (unpublished) ("A claim may be exhausted prior to filing suit or during suit, *so long as exhaustion was completed before the first time the prisoner sought to include the claim in the suit.*") (Emphasis added).

[190] *Hatcher v. Harrington*, No. 14-00554 JMS/KSC, 2015 U.S. Dist. LEXIS 13799, 2015 WL 474313, at *4 (D. Haw. Feb. 5, 2015).

[191] *Hatcher v. Harrington*, No. 14-00554 JMS/KSC, 2015 U.S. Dist. LEXIS 13799, 2015 WL 474313, at *5 (D. Haw. Feb. 5, 2015) (listing cases) ("Nothing in the PREA explicitly or implicitly suggests that Congress intended to create a private right of action for inmates to sue prison officials for noncompliance with the Act.").

[192] *Omaro v. Annucci*, 68 F. Supp. 3d 359, 2014 WL 6068573, at *4 (W.D.N.Y. 2014) ("Nothing in the text or legislative history of the PREA suggests that it was intended to abrogate the PLRA's exhaustion requirement."); *Lamb v. Franke*, No. 2:12-cv-367-MO,

2013 U.S. Dist. LEXIS 22708, 2013 WL 638836, at *2 (D.Or. Feb. 14, 2013) (unpublished) ("The PREA does not impose an alternative remedial scheme, nor does it supersede PLRA's exhaustion requirement.").

[193] JASON KEEL, Plaintiff, vs. CORIZON MEDICAL SERVICES, et al., Defendants. CAUSE NO. 3:14-CV-1492 UNITED STATES DISTRICT COURT FOR THE NORTHERN DISTRICT OF INDIANA, SOUTH BEND DIVISION

[194] *Ford v. Johnson*, 362 F.3d 395, 398 (7th Cir. 2004) ("exhaustion must precede litigation"); *Perez v. Wisconsin Department of Corrections*, 182 F.3d 532, 535 (7th Cir. 1999) (compliance with 42 U.S.C. § 1997e(a) is a "precondition to suit").

[195] *Jones v. Bock*, 549 U.S. 199, 216, 127 S. Ct. 910, 166 L. Ed. 2d 798 (2007); *Dole v. Chandler*, 438 F.3d 804, 809 (7th Cir. 2006).

[196] *Pozo v. McCaughtry*, 286 F.3d 1022, 1025 (7th Cir. 2002).

[197] WILLIAM R. TUBBS, PLAINTIFF v. CORIZON, INC.; et al., DEFENDANTS 5:13CV00377-BSM-JJV UNITED STATES DISTRICT COURT FOR THE EASTERN DISTRICT OF ARKANSAS, PINE BLUFF DIVISION

[198] *See* 42 U.S.C. § 1997e(a); *Jones v. Bock*, 549 U.S. 199, 202, 127 S. Ct. 910, 166 L. Ed. 2d 798 (2007); *Jones v. Norris*, 310 F.3d 610, 612 (8th Cir. 2002).

[199] **HAROLD DAVEY CASSELL ADC # 073885, PLAINTIFF V. CORRECT CARE SOLUTIONS, LLC AND CORIZON, INC., DEFENDANTS 5:14CV00403-DPM-JJV UNITED STATES DISTRICT COURT FOR THE EASTERN DISTRICT OF ARKANSAS, PINE BLUFF DIVISION**

[200] *See* 42 U.S.C. § 1997e(a); *Jones v. Bock*, 549 U.S. 199, 202, 127 S. Ct. 910, 166 L. Ed. 2d 798 (2007); *Jones v. Norris*, 310 F.3d 610, 612 (8th Cir. 2002).

[201]DWAYNE R. STEPHENSON, PLAINTIFF, VS. CORIZON MEDICAL SERVICES, DR. YOUNG, NP POULSON, ET AL., DEFENDANTS. Case No. 1:14-cv-00460-BLW UNITED STATES DISTRICT COURT FOR THE DISTRICT OF IDAHO

[202]Robert Schilleman, Plaintiff, v. Corizon Health Incorporated, et al., Defendants. No. CV 14-01825-PHX-DLR (BSB) UNITED STATES DISTRICT COURT FOR THE DISTRICT OF ARIZONA

[203]*See* 42 U.S.C. § 1997e(a); *Vaden v. Summerhill*, 449 F.3d 1047, 1050 (9th Cir. 2006); *Brown v. Valoff*, 422 F.3d 926, 934-35 (9th Cir. 2005).

[204]*See Woodford v. Ngo*, 548 U.S. 81, 92, 126 S. Ct. 2378, 165 L. Ed. 2d 368 (2006).

[205]*Porter v. Nussle*, 534 U.S. 516, 523, 122 S. Ct. 983, 152 L. Ed. 2d 12 (2002),

[206]*Booth v. Churner*, 532 U.S. 731, 741, 121 S. Ct. 1819, 149 L. Ed. 2d 958 (2001).

[207]*Albino v. Baca*, 747 F.3d 1162, 1169, 1172 (9th Cir. 2014); *see Brown*, 422 F.3d at 936-37 (a defendant must demonstrate that applicable relief remained available in the grievance process).

[208]**Morton v. Hall, 599 F.3d 942, 946 (9th Cir. 2010) (The level of detail in an administrative grievance necessary to properly exhaust a claim is determined by the prison's applicable grievance procedures, but "when a prison's** grievance procedures are silent or incomplete as to factual specificity, a grievance suffices if it alerts the prison to the nature of the wrong for which redress is sought.").

[209]CARL RUPERT SMITH, #137 787, Plaintiff, v. CORIZON HEALTH SERVICES, et al., Defendants. **CIVIL ACTION NO. 2:15-CV-20-MHT UNITED STATES DISTRICT COURT FOR THE**

MIDDLE DISTRICT OF ALABAMA, NORTHERN DIVISION

[210] *Bryant v. Rich*, 530 F.3d 1368, 1374-75 (11th Cir. 2008) (internal quotations omitted); *Trias v. Fla. Dep't of Corr.*, 587 F. App'x 531, 534 (11th Cir. 2014) (District court properly construed defendant's "motion for summary judgment as a motion to dismiss for failure to exhaust administrative remedies").

[211] ***Higginbottom v. Carter*, 223 F.3d 1259, 1261 (11th Cir. 2000) (per curiam) (quoting *Freeman v. Francis*, 196 F.3d 641, 643-44 (6th Cir. 1999)). See id. (affirming dismissal of prisoner's civil rights suit for failure to satisfy the mandatory exhaustion requirements of the PLRA); *Harris v. Garner*, 190 F.3d 1279, 1286 (11th Cir. 1999) ("reaffirm[ing] that *section 1997e(a)* imposes a mandatory requirement on prisoners seeking judicial relief to exhaust their administrative remedies" before filing suit in federal court), *modified on other grounds*, 216 F.3d 970 (11th Cir. 2000) (en banc); *Miller v. Tanner*, 196 F.3d 1190, 1193 (11th Cir. 1999) (holding that under the PLRA's amendments to ~1997e(a)*, "[a]n inmate incarcerated in a state prison . . . must first comply with the grievance procedures established by the state department of corrections before filing a federal lawsuit under *section 1983*"); *Harper v. Jenkin*, 179 F.3d 1311, 1312 (11th Cir. 1999) (per curiam) (affirming dismissal of prisoner's civil suit for failure to satisfy the mandatory exhaustion requirements of ~1997e(a)*); *Alexander v. Hawk*, 159 F.3d 1321, 1328 (11th Cir. 1998) (affirming dismissal of prisoner's *Bivens* action under ~1997e(a)* for failure to exhaust administrative remedies prior to filing suit in federal court).*Leal v. Ga. Dep't of Corr.*, 254 F.3d 1276, 1279 (11th Cir. 2001).

[212] *Chandler v. Crosby*, 379 F.3d 1278, 1286 (11th Cir. 2004). Because exhaustion is mandated by the statute, [a court has] no discretion to waive this requirement. *Alexander v. Hawk*, 159 F.3d 1321,

1325-26 (11th Cir. 1998)." *Myles v. Miami-Dade Cnty. Corr. and Rehab. Dep't*, 476 F. App'x 364, 366 (11th Cir. 2012).

[213] *Turner v. Burnside*, 541 F.3d 1077, 1082 (11th Cir. 2008) (*citing Bryant*, 530 F.3d at 1373-74).

[214] *Booth v. Churner*, 532 U.S. 731, 741 n.6, 121 S. Ct. 1819, 149 L. Ed. 2d 958 (2001).

[215] *Porter v. Nussle*, 534 U.S. 516, 532, 122 S. Ct. 983, 152 L. Ed. 2d 12 (2002).

[216] *Booth*, 532 U.S. at 741; *Alexander*, 159 F.3d at 1325; *Woodford v. Ngo*, 548 U.S. 81, 126 S. Ct. 2378, 165 L. Ed. 2d 368 (2006).

[217] *Smith v. Terry*, 491 F. App'x 81, 83 (11th Cir. 2012) (per curiam).

[218] JAMES COLEN #604910, Plaintiff, v. CORIZON MEDICAL SERVICES, et al., Defendants. Civil **Action No.: 14-12948 UNITED STATES DISTRICT COURT FOR THE EASTERN DISTRICT OF MICHIGAN, SOUTHERN DIVISION**

[219] We discuss the decisions as written by the judges with modification for emphasis.

[220] **KEVIN** Mitchell**, PLAINTIFF, V. CORIZON HEALTH, INC., ET AL., DEFENDANTS.** *2015 U.S. Dist. LEXIS 9759 (*January 28, 2015)

[221] **JOHN KRISTOFFER LARSGARD, PLAINTIFF, VS. CORIZON HEALTH, INC., DEFENDANT**. 2014 U.S. Dist. LEXIS 150333 (October 21, 2014)

[222] *In re Homestore.com., Inc. v. Sec. Litig.*, 347 F. Supp. 2d 769, 782 (C.D. Cal. 2004) (**finding print outs from a web site inadmissible at summary judgment because they were not properly authenticated by an affidavit from someone with knowledge**); *see also Barcamerica Int'l USA Trust v. Tyfield Imps., Inc.*, 289 F.3d 589, 593 n. 4 (9th Cir. 2002) ("arguments and statements of counsel are not evidence") (internal quotation omitted).

²²³EDWARD **ALLEN MOORE, PLAINTIFF, V. CORIZON, LLC, DEFENDANT.** No. 4:15-CV-597 RLW UNITED STATES DISTRICT COURT FOR THE EASTERN DISTRICT OF MISSOURI, EASTERN DIVISION

²²⁴**WILLIAM R. TUBBS, PLAINTIFF V. CORIZON, INC.; ET AL., DEFENDANTS** 5:13CV00377-BSM-JJV UNITED STATES DISTRICT COURT FOR THE EASTERN DISTRICT OF ARKANSAS, PINE BLUFF DIVISION

²²⁵**Dulany v. Carnahan, 132 F.3d 1234, 1240 (8th Cir.1997) ("In the face of medical records indicating that treatment was provided and physician affidavits indicating that the care provided was adequate, an inmate cannot create a question of fact by merely stating that she did not feel she received adequate treatment.")**

²²⁶**JIMMIE L. SIMPSON, PLAINTIFF, V. CORIZON HEALTH, INC. ET AL., DEFENDANTS.** Case No. 1:15-cv-357 UNITED STATES DISTRICT COURT FOR THE WESTERN DISTRICT OF MICHIGAN, SOUTHERN DIVISION

²²⁷DONALD RAY PALMER, PLAINTIFF, VS. CORIZON INCORPORATED, ET AL., DEFENDANTS. **No. CV 14-8013-PCT-DGC (MHB) UNITED STATES DISTRICT COURT FOR THE DISTRICT OF ARIZONA**

²²⁸CRAIG DOMINIC BENACQUISTO, PLAINTIFF, VS. CORIZON HEALTH, ET AL., DEFENDANTS. **No. CV 13-2309-PHX-DGC (MEA) UNITED STATES DISTRICT COURT FOR THE DISTRICT OF ARIZONA**

www.ingramcontent.com/pod-product-compliance
Lightning Source LLC
Chambersburg PA
CBHW051539020426
42333CB00016B/2011